Functional Parametrization Hypothesis
in the Minimalist Program:
Case Studies from the Perspective of Comparative Syntax
of Japanese and English

JN062018

Functional Parametrization Hypothesis in the Minimalist Program:

Case Studies from the Perspective of Comparative Syntax of Japanese and English

Ryoichiro Kobayashi

KAITAKUSHA

Kaitakusha Co., Ltd.
22–16, Otowa 1-chome
Bunkyo-ku, Tokyo 112–0013
Japan

Functional Parametrization Hypothesis in the Minimalist Program:
Case Studies from the Perspective of Comparative Syntax of Japanese and English

Published in Japan
by Kaitakusha Co., Ltd., Tokyo

Copyright © 2022
by Ryoichiro Kobayashi

All rights reserved. No part of this publication may be
reproduced, stored in a retrieval system, or transmitted,
in any form or by any means, electronic, mechanical,
photocopying, recording, or otherwise, without the prior
permission of the copyright owner.

First published 2022

Printed and bound in Japan
by Hinode Printing Co., Ltd.

Cover design by Shihoko Nakamura

Preface

This book is a modified version of my doctoral dissertation (Kobayashi 2022) submitted to the Graduate School of Languages and Linguistics at Sophia University. First, I am extremely grateful to the members of my doctoral dissertation committee, Naoki Fukui (chairperson), Takaomi Kato, Toru Ishii, and Hiroki Narita. I am also deeply indebted to the following linguists for their support and encouragement: Asako Uchibori, Hisatsugu Kitahara, Mihoko Zushi, Ryan Walter Smith, Takanobu Nakamura, and Yushi Sugimoto. Special thanks go to Takakazu Nagamori, who helped me immensely by proofreading the earlier version of this manuscript.

Chapter 2 of this book is an extended and radically revised version of Kobayashi (2018a), which was presented at the 13th Workshop on Altaic Formal Linguistics (WAFL 13) and at *Keio Gengogaku Kenkyuukai* (Keio Study Group of Linguistics) both held in Tokyo. Chapter 3 grew out of Kobayashi (2018b), a part of which was originally presented at the workshop titled "Current Issues in Comparative Minimalist Syntax," at the 34th Annual Meeting of The English Linguistic Society of Japan held in Kanazawa, and at ConSOLE XXV held in Leipzig. Some portions of the dissertation (Kobayashi 2022) were also presented at the Keio Linguistic Colloquium held online on April 23rd, 2022. I would like to thank the organizers and audiences there for their valuable comments.

The project of this book was partially financially supported by the Japan

Society for the Promotion of Science (JSPS) KAKENHI Grant-in-Aid for JSPS Fellows JP16J00637, Grant-in-Aid for Early-Career Scientists JP19K13228, and Grant-in-Aid for Scientific Research (C) JP21K00574, for which I am extremely grateful.

Finally, I would like to thank my family members, especially my parents, Shunsuke and Hitomi for their encouragement. Last, but not least, my deepest gratitude goes to my wife Yuko, who has always been by my side and together with whom I have overcome countless hardships. I dedicate this book to her.

Contents

Functional Parametrization Hypothesis in the Minimalist Program:

Case Studies from the Perspective of Comparative Syntax of Japanese and English

Chapter 1

Introduction

1.1. Outline of Chapter 1

The aim of this book is to argue that Japanese lacks [uφ], and that the presence / absence of agreement features yields certain parametric variation, which is part of the Functional Parametrization Hypothesis (**FPH**: Fukui 1986 / 1995, 1988, 1995 *inter alia*). Recently, Chomsky (2010), Berwick and Chomsky (2011, 2016), and Boeckx (2011, 2014, 2016), among others, have argued for the Externalization Hypothesis (**EH**), which states that cross-linguistic variation only arises at the PF-branch / externalization. Chapter 1 states that it is reasonable that some cross-linguistic variation stems from the presence / absence of certain agreement features (i.e., φ-features) of functional categories.

In this chapter, I aim to contextualize the proposal made in this book in the larger framework of linguistic theory, namely in the debate on the locus of linguistic variation. This introductory chapter provides conceptual and empirical support of the claim that some functional categories, unlike lexical categories, are subject to variation (Fukui 1988, 1995, among others). By reviewing the literature on the different approaches to the study of language in Section 1.3, we find that functional categories are empirically different from lexical categories because they are acquired later (Language Acquisition) and are subject to disappearance (Language Disorder: agrammatism). I conclude that functional categories are empirically distinct from lexical categories. The discussion is followed by the proposal of this book. I argue for the following statement, which is part of the FPH in (1) proposed by Fukui (1988, 1990, 1995) and Chomsky (1995):

(1)   **The Agreement Parametrization Hypothesis:**
      The presence / absence of agreement features of functional categories in the lexicon yields certain parametric variation.

Specifically, I argue that Japanese lacks [uφ] in its lexicon (Fukui 1986 / 1995, 1988, Saito 2007, 2016, among many others) and demonstrate that adopting this argument explains certain differences between Japanese and other languages, especially English.

In Section 1.4, I argue that lexical categories are primary in the design of human language compared to functional categories for the following reason: language is primarily designed as an instrument of thought (Chomsky 2007a); hence, lexical categories, which serve as basic units of thought and provide predicate-argument structure in LF (Fukui and Sakai 2003), are the core ingredients in the human language. Functional categories, which lack substantive semantic content, are secondary in human language. By analogy, with an example of genetic variation from general biology (Lewontin 1985), I argue that lexical categories are invariant across languages, while functional categories are subject to variation.

Thereafter, I argue that it is reasonable to assume variation in the presence / absence of agreement features of functional categories across languages. Overall, this book provides a counterargument to the strict version of the EH, which presumes that there is no variation in the presyntactic lexicon (Chomsky 2010, Berwick and Chomsky 2011, 2016, Boeckx 2011, 2014, 2016).

(2)   **The Externalization Hypothesis (EH):**
      Cross-linguistic differences only arise in the PF-branch.

(Boeckx 2016)

Let us commence with the discussion on linguistic variations and lexical / functional categories.

1.2.   Lexical vs. Functional Categories

I first summarize the discussion of parameters and lexical / functional categories in the history of Generative Grammar. Under the Principles and
Parameters (**P&P**) approach, Language Acquisition comprises fixing a limited
number of parameter values associated with the principles in UG. The early
P&P theory assumed that all parameters were about the principles of Universal
Grammar. Thus, they were attributed to the innate properties of the Faculty
of Language. This view has changed significantly since then. Early P&P did
not answer the question about the kinds of parameters that were possible or
impossible. Apart from stating that all parameters were grammatical parameters, no formal property was provided to delineate the range of possible
parameters. Therefore, the question of how to delimit the class of available
parameters arose.

In this context, Borer (1984) proposes that parametric variation is limited
to the inflectional properties of languages. Wexler and Manzini (1987) (see
also Manzini and Wexler 1987) refine Borer's idea to propose that the parameter setting should be linked with the acquisition of lexical items in each
language. This is called the *Lexical Parametrization Hypothesis* (**LPH**: Yang
1983, Vikner 1985, Manzini and Wexler 1987, Wexler and Manzini 1987,
Baker 1988, 2003, Newson 1990, among others), as stated in (3) below:

(3)   **The Lexical Parametrization Hypothesis (LPH):**
      Values of a parameter are associated not with particular languages,
      but with particular lexical items in a language.

                                          (Wexler and Manzini 1987: 55)

Through observations of binding in English and Icelandic, Wexler and
Manzini (1987) attempt to provide an answer to what the learnable (hence,
possible) parameters in human languages are. A novelty and the moot point
of the approach is the assumption that parameters are set for each lexical item
(Naoki Fukui p.c.). In an extreme case, this should allow for more parameters
than the number of lexical items in a language. As Safir (1987: 79–80) indicates, parameters as defined by Wexler and Manzini (1987) are incompatible
with minimizing the number of crosslinguistic parameters.

Around the same time, another dominant view appeared in the theory that attempted to limit the class of possible parameters. Fukui (1988) proposes that the locus of cross-linguistic parametric differences is restricted to functional categories. This is the *Functional Parametrization Hypothesis* (**FPH**: Fukui 1986/1995, 1988, 1995, 2006, among others), as described in (4) below:

(4)   **The Functional Parameterization Hypothesis (FPH):**[1]
       Values of a parameter are associated not with particular languages, but with functional elements in the lexicon.
                            (adapted from Fukui 1988: 266–269, 1995: 342–343)

The FPH is conceptually preferable to the LPH in that only the former strictly restricts the set of possible parameters in the theory of language.[2]

1.3.   Language Acquisition and Language Disorder

It is possible to *conceptually* distinguish functional categories from lexical categories. A question that arises is whether functional categories can be *empirically* distinguished from lexical categories. By reviewing the literature on different approaches to the study of language, we find that functional categories are empirically distinguishable from lexical categories in the lexicon since they are acquired later (Language Acquisition) and are subject to loss (Language Disorder: agrammatism).

---

[1] Fukui (1988, 1995) implies that the Head Parameter is the only independent Macro-parameter that exists in UG. Fukui's (1988, 1995) original statements regarding a restrictive theory of parametric variation of Fukui (1988, 1995) are as follows:

(i) a.   Parametric variation outside of the lexicon must be limited to ordering restrictions ('linearity').
    b.   Inside the lexicon, only functional elements are subject to parametric variation.
    c.   Among the functional elements, only those that do not play any role in LF can be absent in the lexicon of a particular language.
                            (Fukui 1988: 266–269, 1995: 342–343)

[2] Baker (2003: 4) claims that there is variation in lexical categories as well. For instance, he observes Mohawk and argues that it lacks adjectival categories. This could provide a piece of counterevidence to the FPH. However, I leave this issue for future research.

1.3.1.   Language Acquisition and Functional Categories

Lebeaux (1988, 2000), Radford (1988, 1990), Platzack (1990), Poeppel and
Wexler (1993), Wexler (1998), Crain and Lillo-Martin (1999), Potts and
Roeper (2006), and Thornton and Tesan (2007), among many others, state that
in a developmental stage of children's language ability, their utterances lack
functional categories. Categories such as D, T (originally, I), and C are acquired later in what Radford calls the functional stage (Radford 1988, 1990).

Radford (1990: 54) claims that the categorial component of early child
grammars in English is lexical. There are three stages in Language
Acquisition regarding the presence of functional and lexical categories: (i) the
precategorial stage, (ii) the lexical stage, and (iii) the functional stage.
Children's utterances are acategorial in the precategorial stage. In the lexical
stage, they combine words of lexical categories. Evidence is in children's im-
itation of adults' utterances in (5). All the words imitated belong to lexical
categories, whereas omitted items belong to functional categories. At the age
of 24 months ±20%, children produce evidence of functional categories
(Radford 1990: 48). According to Radford (1988, 1990), early child grammar
has the traits demonstrated in (6).

(5) a.   ADULT: Mr. Miller will try.
        CHILD: Miller try.
        (Susan 24)
    b.   ADULT: I will read the book.
        CHILD: Read book.
        (Eve 25)

(Radford 1990: 55)

(6)   Some characteristic traits of early child grammar:
    a.   Child clauses lack complementizers.
    b.   Child clauses have no subject auxiliary inversion.
    c.   Child clauses have no preposed *wh*-phrases.
    d.   Child clauses lack infinitival *to*.
    e.   Child clauses lack modal auxiliaries.
    f.   Child clauses have negation by particles (*no* / *not*), not by auxil-
       iaries.
    g.   Child clauses lack verbs marked for Tense.

h.   Child clauses lack verbs marked for agreement.

i.   Child clauses lack mastery of nominative case assignment.

(Radford 1988: 27–28)

The early-stage language of children lacks agreement features, since these features are related to the functional heads that are acquired in the later functional stage. The fact that functional categories and agreement features are acquired later than lexical categories during Language Acquisition indicates that lexical categories should be empirically distinguished from functional categories.

Lebeaux (2000: 155), among others, mentions that one might object to the above conclusion since a functional explanation could be provided. Children have limited (working) memory in their early language development stages. Syntactic structures are created in a bottom-up manner. Therefore, one might say that given such performative limitations, functional categories are not produced by young children since they are structurally higher than lexical categories: young children, with limited working memory, can have functional categories in their inventory but cannot construct the complete syntactic structures with them because of processing failure. I call this explanation a functionalist approach and will demonstrate that this counterargument cannot hold using the following two observations.

First, Lillo-Martin (1994: 310–312) argues against such a functionalist approach. She conducted a longitudinal study of the acquisition of American Sign Language (**ASL**) by deaf children of different ages. She observes two groups of deaf children: a group of younger deaf children of about two years old and a group of older deaf children of around five to nine years old. The parents of the deaf children in the latter group were not native signers, and their children acquired ASL from native signers at a later age. Therefore, their general language-independent cognitive abilities were more developed when they went through the early stages of Language Acquisition than the former group of children.

Lillo-Martin (1994: 311) primarily studies the use of null arguments in ASL, but also observes that the latter group of children underwent stages without functional elements / inflectional properties.[3] Since the cognitive ca-

---

[3] What is considered as a functional element depends on the analysis of ASL. I follow

pacities of the older deaf children are likely to be far more mature than those of the younger children of around two years old, the fact that they underwent pre-functional stages before entering the functional stage strongly indicates that working memory or processing ability is irrelevant to the lack of functional categories in early child grammar. Supposing that Lillo-Martin's (1994) observation is correct, this discussion serves as a counterargument to the functionalist approach mentioned above.

Second, Jordens (2002) argues against the functionalist approach to the lack of functional categories in early child grammar. He notes that young children do not use complementizers in the pre-functional stages. He argues that this is not because of a limited working memory or processing capacity. It has been widely observed that young children in the pre-functional stages produce embedded clauses in Dutch (Jordens 2002: 690). However, these clauses systematically lack complementizers, which cannot be omitted in adult Dutch grammar, as illustrated in (7).

(7)   The lack of null complementizers in adult Dutch grammar:
    a.   Vroeg je   nou of die plaats vrij is
        asked you now if that seat   free is
        (of dat   ie bezet is).
        or   that it taken is
        Lit. 'Did you ask if that the seat is free (or that the seat is taken)?'
    b.   *Vroeg je   nou of Ø   plaats vrij is
        asked you now if that seat   free is
        (of Ø   ie bezet is).
        or   that it taken is
    c.   Hij zei [dat/*Ø Jan   Komt] het feest wel
        he   said that   John comes the party no-doubt
        zal   opluisteren.
        will enhance
        'He said that John's coming will certainly enhance the party.'
                (adapted from Neeleman and van de Koot 2006: 697–698)

Lillo-Martin (1994) and assume that ASL shows agreement and has functional elements. I thank Asako Uchibori (p.c.) for pointing this out to me.

The fact that early child grammar in Dutch produces embedded clauses without functional categories suggests that their exclusion is a principled one, not just a functional one concerning working memory or processing ability. This supports the absence of functional categories in pre-categorial and lexical stages (Radford 1988, 1990).[4]

In summary, there are several counterarguments to the functionalist approach. Therefore, it is reasonable to claim that early child grammar lacks functional categories in the lexicon. The findings of Language Acquisition studies indicate that lexical categories must be empirically distinguished from functional categories.

1.3.2.   Language Disorder (Agrammatism) and Functional Categories

In this section, I focus on agrammatism (Grodzinsky 1984, Hagiwara 1995). The speech of agrammatic patients usually consists of lexical categories, while functional categories are not attested (Friedmann and Grodzinsky 1997). Language Disorder studies in the 1980s claimed that agrammatic speech lacked any functional categories (Grodzinsky 1984). Grodzinsky (1984: 106) claims that agrammatic patients omit free grammatical morphemes, such as determiners and auxiliaries. Later, researchers found that agrammatism is a matter of degree: certain functional elements and agreement features are lost in agrammatic patients' speech according to the severity of the symptoms (Friedmann and Grodzinsky 1997). In principle, functional categories disappear from the speech of agrammatic patients while lexical categories do not. Based on these observations, it is natural to conclude that functional categories need to be empirically distinguished from lexical categories in the lexicon since only the former are subject to disappearance.

Similar to the case of Language Acquisition in Section 1.3.1, a functionalist approach to the lack of functional categories seems compatible with the observations of agrammatism. That is, due to deficits in working memory, agrammatic patients cannot produce functional categories, as they are structurally higher than lexical categories. I argue against such functionalist approaches by reviewing two different observations of agrammatism.

First, Thompson et al. (2002) conducted qualitative research on an

---

[4] Note that V2 movement is absent in early child Dutch (Jordens 2002: 689).

agrammatic patient. The patient was diagnosed as having no problem with working memory (Thompson et al. 2002: 193). They found that their patient produced complex structures with embedding, such as relative clauses with a relative pronoun *who*, such as *boy who stalk her*.[5] Significantly, the patient's speech completely lacked the properties of T (i.e., Tense, Aspect, auxiliaries, and agreement features). The patient's knowledge of lexical categories remained intact throughout the study. Since the patient had no working memory deficit, the complete lack of properties of T in the patient's production indicates that working memory deficits may not be crucial for the absence of functional categories.

Second, Penke (1998, 2000), Wenzlaff and Clahsen (2005), and Clahsen (2008) report that the verb-second (**V2**) order is preserved in their German-speaking patients, who were diagnosed as agrammatic. Here, I focus on Wenzlaff and Clahsen (2005), who conducted production tasks in German with their seven agrammatic patients, who are likely to have memory deficits (see Fiebach et al. 2005). In German, V2 movement occurs only in the matrix clause, as in (8). It is widely accepted that German V2 movement is an instance of verb movement to the functional C-domain (Wurmbrand 2000, among others). Placing an adverb sentence-initially, these patients produced complex sentences with correct V2 movement in German. They observe that the speech of their patients lacked T properties (i.e., Tense, Aspect, auxiliaries, and agreement features), but six out of the seven patients had high overall accuracy scores for V2 movement.[6]

(8) V2 in German:
   Gestern   **sagte** er [dass es drau*ß*en nicht sicher ist].
   Yesterday **said** he that it outside not safe is
   'Yesterday, he said it is not safe outside.'

(Ito 2018: 1)

Since the German V2 movement is to the C-domain (Wurmbrand 2000,

---

[5] One may wonder where the relative pronoun *who* is in the structure. Although the patient's speech lacks the properties of T, I assume that there is C in the structure and that *who* remains in [Spec, CP]. In other words, I assume that C is merged with *v*/VP without T in the patient's grammar.

[6] The other patient's accuracy score for V2 movement was significantly higher than the chance level.

among others), that V2 order is maintained in the agrammatic patients' speech indicates that they have C but lack properties of T. Since syntactic structure is created in a bottom-up fashion, this fact is unexpected under the functionalist approach. Such an approach predicts that the agrammatic language lacks only (i) C or (ii) C and T together, but not (iii) lacking only T. Such systematic absence, only of T, in the agrammatic patients' speech can serve as another counterargument to the functionalist approach.[7] In conclusion, there are several counterarguments to the functionalist approach. Thus, it is reasonable to argue that the agrammatic language lacks functional categories. Observations of Language Disorder (agrammatism) studies imply that lexical categories must be empirically distinguished from functional categories.

1.3.3. Interim Conclusion

Discussions on Language Acquisition and Language Disorder indicate that functional categories are empirically distinct from lexical categories. In the next section, I assert that they differ essentially in their functions in the design of human language: lexical categories are the basic units to express human thought (Fukui 1988), as such, they are invariant across languages, while functional categories are secondary in the design of human language, and thus they are subject to variation.

1.4. Lexical Categories and Language as a System of Thought

Fukui (1988) states that lexical categories are the basic units for expression of

---

[7] One might object to the above conclusion by arguing that the German V2 movement is not V-to-C but rather V-to-T. However, such a counterargument does not hold. As illustrated in the German sentence in (8), V2 movement occurs in the matrix clause, but not in the embedded clause in German. The lack of V2 movement in the embedded clause is attributed to the obligatory presence of a complementizer in German embedded clauses (cf. Wurmbrand 2000, among others). In German, C must be occupied by some element. Since C is already occupied by an overt complementizer, the verbal element does not move to C. If the German V2 movement were an instance of V-to-T movement, V2 orders would be derived regardless of the presence of an overt complementizer in the embedded clause. However, this is not the case. Therefore, I conclude that the German V2 movement is an instance of movement to the C-domain.

thought (Fukui 1988: 267). The functions of functional categories are different from those of lexical categories.[8] Their basic role is to introduce agreement features and induce syntactic agreement. Moreover, some of them, such as C and T, contribute to the duality of semantics. Agreement features are LF-uninterpretable and irrelevant to LF or human thought. In this book, I focus on unvalued φ-features and argue that Japanese lacks them in its lexicon.

1.4.1. Functions of Functional Categories

Here, I focus on two functions of functional categories in human languages: (i) contribution to the duality of semantics, and (ii) introduction of agreement features. First, some functional categories, such as C and T, contribute to the duality of semantics. External Merge yields the argument structure, while internal Merge yields the discourse-related structure, such as new / old information, focus, and interrogative constructions (Chomsky 2014). The C and T heads create the C-T domain, in which discourse-related information is expressed. This function seems to be necessary for all languages since the duality of semantics is observed universally. Thus, I assume that functional features that contribute to the duality of semantics (i.e., operator-variable / topic-comment features) are highly likely to be universal across languages.

Second, functional categories are the loci of agreement features (Fukui 1986 / 1995, 1988, 1995, Muysken 2008, among others). Functional categories introduce unvalued features to syntactic derivations. I argue that this function is not universally attested and that certain unvalued features need not be present in a language. Specifically, I focus on [uφ] and argue that Japanese lacks [uφ] in its lexicon. In this book, I aim to demonstrate several empirical consequences of this proposal.

---

[8] One obvious question concerns the categorial status of small v in the theory. This head introduces an external argument (a lexical property) but has no substantive semantic content (a functional property). Chomsky (2000, 2001, 2008, *inter alia*) leaves it open whether v is a functional or lexical head. I assume with Travis (2014), among others, that small v is neither functional nor lexical, but is semi-functional. The discussions in Chapter 3 may imply that the small v is perhaps functional in that it introduces φ-features to the derivation, which are inherited by V. In this book, I leave it open whether small v is lexical or functional in nature.

1.4.2. Primary vs. Secondary Categories and Variation in a System

Fukui and Sakai (2003: 324) argue that lexical categories have substantive content, which eventually leads to the construction of a predicate-argument structure at LF.[9] Functional categories, on the other hand, do not have such substantive content. Fukui (1988: 267) claims that "[i]t is quite inconceivable that a language without lexical categories, the basic units of expression, can serve as a free instrument of thought and self-expression, an oft-cited function of human language." Functional categories do not have their own semantic meaning parallel to that of lexical categories; hence, it is possible to form a basic unit of thought (i.e., predicate-argument structure) without functional categories (Fukui and Sakai 2003: 324). Since it is understood that human language is optimally designed primarily as an instrument of thought (Chomsky 2007a), I argue that in this respect lexical categories are primary within the design of human language.

Furthermore, I argue that it is reasonable that functional categories are subject to variation in contrast to lexical categories. Let us consider how be-ing primary / secondary to the biological system / design relates to (in)variation. Characters that are not crucial for life-maintenance are secondary in the whole system / design and subject to genetic variation (cf. Lewontin 1985: 79–80, among others). These characters include skin and eye colors and types of hair (Walsh 2003: 285, Otsuka 2007: 37, and Nakao 2012: 2, 2013: 12, among others). On the other hand, traits that are crucial for life-maintenance, for in-stance, traits of the heart and lungs, are in principle not subject to genetic variation among humans. Through this analogy, I maintain that it is reason-able to assume that crucial / primary parts in a system of living creatures are not subject to variation, while the secondary parts are subject to variation.

It is undeniable that there are variations in human languages. Moreover, human language is an organ (Chomsky 1980). Therefore, it is not unnatural to attribute these variations to functional categories, which are secondary in the system of human language. In summary, I argue that the analogy from general biology suggests that the primary lexical categories are not subject to variation, while there are variations in functional categories, which are second-

---

[9] I assume that modification by (attributive) adjectives is also a part of the basic unit of human thought.

ary in the human thought system.

Among the functional elements, some play a role in the human thought system (Naoki Fukui p.c.). For instance, Tense (taking an event) may play substantive roles in the human thought system beyond the predicate-argument structure. This functional element, whether or not it appears as a syntactic head in the computation of narrow syntax, can be universal and might not be susceptible to variation in human languages.[10] Among the functional elements, unvalued φ-features are LF-uninterpretable and do not play any role in the human thought system. Therefore, I focus on unvalued φ-features in this book.[11]

1.4.3. Proposal

As agreement features relate to functional categories, it is reasonable to assume that there is variation among them. It is widely assumed that LF is uniform across languages (Chomsky and Lasnik 1993). Certain agreement features (e.g., [uφ]) are LF-uninterpretable; hence, it is natural to seek cross-linguistic variation in them (Fukui 1990: 268–269). Assuming this is correct, it is natural to claim that a language may lack [uφ] in the lexicon.

I situate the proposal in this book within the larger framework of linguistic theory to explain certain cross-linguistic differences and support the claim that there is variation in agreement features in the lexicon. Therefore, this book presents a counterargument to the EH described in (9) (Chomsky 2010, Berwick and Chomsky 2011, 2016, Boeckx 2011, 2014, 2016, among others).

(9) **The Externalization Hypothesis (EH)**:
Cross-linguistic differences only arise in the PF-branch.

(Boeckx 2016)

---

[10] Even if a language has some functional features in its lexicon, it is unclear whether that element crystalizes as a syntactic head in the computation of narrow syntax. There could be variation among languages regarding whether a functional feature, such as Tense and Q-related features, realizes as a syntactic head (Naoki Fukui p.c.). For instance, a Q-feature realizes as a syntactic head -*ka* / *no* 'Q' in Japanese, whereas there is no such particle in English.

[11] Like [uφ], [uCase] is LF-uninterpretable and irrelevant to the human thought system. Therefore, languages may also vary in the presence / absence of [uCase] in narrow syntax (Naoki Fukui and Toru Ishii p.c.). As this issue is beyond the scope of this book, which focuses on [uφ], I leave this for future research.

Boeckx (2016) argues that the theory of the lexicon is undeveloped; hence, it is not desirable to relegate explanations of language variations to the lexicon.[12] Boeckx (2014) criticizes the LPH and the FPH as lexiconcentric. Assuming that narrow syntax is uniform, he proposes the Strong Uniformity Thesis (**SUT**), presented in (10), which consists of two parts.

(10)   Strong Uniformity Thesis (SUT):
        Principles of narrow syntax are not subject to parametrization; nor are they affected by lexical parameters.
                            (Boeckx 2011: 210, 2014: 119, 2016: 73)

Under the FPH (or the LPH), syntactic variation can arise in current Minimalist models via the influence of pre-syntactic differences in the lexicon. Boeckx (2014, 2016) emphasizes that this is true only because current Minimalist models of narrow syntax are lexiconcentric.

In this chapter, I argued that there can be variation in agreement features of functional categories. By reviewing the literature on Language Acquisition (Section 1.3.1) and Language Disorder (Section 1.3.2), I concluded that functional categories are empirically different from lexical categories. Furthermore, I contended that functional categories are secondary in the design of human language by carefully reviewing differences in their functions in language. As functional categories are secondary, it is natural to claim that they and their agreement features are subject to variation, unlike lexical categories. In summary, the discussions in this chapter strongly indicate variation in agreement features of functional categories, although many researchers have pursued the possibilities of the EH and the SUT in the current Minimalist program.

Considering this, and based on the FPH (Fukui 1990, 2013, Chomsky 2015a), I argue for the following statement:

(11)   **The Agreement Parametrization Hypothesis:** (=1)
        The presence / absence of agreement features of functional categories in the lexicon yields certain parametric variation.

---

[12] I deem the theory of externalization un / under-developed. Hence, it is unclear whether it is preferable to relegate the explanations of language variation to externalization than to the lexicon without a concrete discussion of Boeckx's (2016) proposal.

Specifically, I argue that Japanese lacks [uφ] in its lexicon (Fukui 1986/1995, 1988, Saito 2007, 2016, among many others) by examining a couple of differences between Japanese and other languages, particularly English, in Chapters 2, 3, and 4.

1.5.   Review of Previous Studies on the FPH (Fukui 1986/1995, 1988, 1995)

Before we proceed to the next chapter, I review Fukui's (1986/1995, 1988, 1995) influential works on the FPH. Fukui proposes that functional categories close lexical projections: functional categories turn open single-bar level projections of lexical categories into the closed double-bar level projection of functional categories with a SPEC position. For instance, I(NFL) turns the open verbal projection into I′ with a SPEC, which is consequently closed as an I″. This is accomplished via SPEC-Head agreement.

Fukui (1986/1995) assumes that Japanese lacks the class of functional categories (Fukui 1988: 259) except for a very defective INFL. This assumption is immediately followed by several consequent assumptions, including the lack of agreement in Japanese as certain features of functional categories induce agreement (Fukui 1988: 260). Fukui (1988) lists numerous cross-linguistic differences between Japanese and English, presented in (12). In this chapter, I focus on (12d) and (12e) and briefly review them in Sections 1.5.1 and 1.5.2.

(12)   A non-exhaustive list of cross-linguistic differences between Japanese and English:
   a.   English has obligatory syntactic *wh* movement, while Japanese does not.
   b.   English has overt expletive elements, while Japanese does not.
   c.   English has subject-auxiliary inversion, while Japanese does not.
   d.   Japanese has multiple subject constructions, while English does not.
   e.   Japanese has (multiple) scrambling, while English does not.
   f.   Japanese has productive complex predicate formation, while English does not.

1.5.1. Multiple Subject Constructions

Japanese clauses are open lexical projections (i.e., V' and N'), as there are no functional categories that close them (Fukui 1986/1995, 1988). Multiple nominative/genitive-marked nominals may appear in the structure, as they can iteratively adjoin to the open lexical projections. The data are presented in (13). This is not the case with English. As there is only one position for the subject, in the SPEC of IP/DP, there can be only one subject in IP/DP. Undeniably, the corresponding English expressions are ungrammatical as in (14).

(13) a.   Bummeikoku-ga   dansei-ga heikinjumyoo-ga
           developed.countries-NOM men-NOM average.longevity-NOM
           mijika-i.
           short-PRES
           Lit. 'Developed countries, men, average longevity is short.'
                                                          (Kuno 1973: 34)
     b.   MIT-de-no senshuu-no   Chomsky-no so-no   koogi
           MIT-at-GEN last.week-GEN Chomsky-GEN that-GEN lecture
           Lit. 'MIT's last week's Chomsky's that lecture'
                                                          (Fukui 1988: 257)

(14) a.   *Civilized countries, male, the average lifespan is short.
     b.   *MIT's last week's Chomsky's that lecture
                                                          (Fukui 1988: 257)

1.5.2. (Multiple) Scrambling

The logic from the previous section of multiple subjects applies to the presence and absence of (multiple) scrambling in Japanese and English, respectively. Japanese clauses are open lexical projections; therefore, there are multiple adjoined positions for preposed nominals (Fukui 1986/1995, 1988). The freely scrambled orders in Japanese are depicted in (15). On the other hand, only one element can be preposed via topicalization in English, which takes place only once per clause (Fukui 1988: 262). Therefore, the corresponding English expressions are all ungrammatical, as presented in (16).

(15) a. Mary-ga   John-ni   so-no   hon-o   watashi-ta.
         Mary-NOM   John-DAT   that-GEN book-ACC give-PAST
         'Mary gave the book to John.'

  b. John-ni$_i$ Mary-ga t_i so-no hon-o watashi-ta.

  c. So-no hon-o$_i$ Mary-ga   John-ni t_i watashi-ta.

  d. So-no hon-o$_j$ John-ni$_i$ Mary-ga t_i t_j watashi-ta.

  e. John-ni$_j$ so-no hon-o$_i$ Mary-ga t_i t_j watashi-ta.

                                                   (Fukui 1988: 257)

(16) a. John put that book on the table.

  b. *On the table$_j$, that book$_i$, John put t_i t_j.

  c. *That book$_j$, on the table$_i$, John put t_i t_j.

  cf. Topicalization:

       (i) That book$_i$, John put t_i on the table.

       (ii) On the table$_j$, John put that book t_j.

                                                   (Fukui 1988: 257)

Fukui's (1986 / 1995, 1988, 1995) previous studies assumed that Japanese lacks functional categories. Although I argue for a part of the FPH in this book in (11), my argument does not necessarily require the lack of functional categories in Japanese. I assume that Japanese has T and C but crucially lacks unvalued φ-features in the lexicon.

1.6. Review of a Previous Study on the Lack of [uφ] in Japanese (Saito 2007)

In this section, I review one of the studies that assume that Japanese lacks φ-features (Saito 2007). In Japanese, Argument Ellipsis (**AE**) is available, as illustrated in (17).[13] (17b) presents the sloppy reading: *Hanako thinks that she washed a car*. On the other hand, the strict reading is: *Hanako thinks that Taro washed a car*. The sloppy reading may imply that the embedded null subject is not a referential *pro* but derived via AE.

---

[13] I leave the discussion open on whether the sloppy reading is obtained via AE or by *pro* (see Hoji 1998 and Saito 2007 for discussions).

(17) a. Taro-wa [zibun-ga kuruma-o araw-ta   to]
         Taro-TOP self-NOM car-ACC   wash-PAST that
         omow-tei-ru.
         think-ASP-PRES
         Lit. 'Taro thinks that himself washed the car.'
     b. Hanako-mo   [*e* kuruma-o araw-ta   to]
         Hanako-also   car-ACC wash-PAST that
         omow-tei-ru.
         think-ASP-PRES
         Lit. 'Hanako also thinks that *e* washed the car.'

$$(^{ok}\text{sloppy reading})$$

Saito (2007), following Oku (1998) and Kim (1999), assumes that AE is implemented via LF-copying, an operation that copies the contents of an antecedent to the null nominal in the ellipsis site. To explain the presence / absence of AE from a comparative perspective, he proposes the Anti-Agreement Hypothesis (**AAH**), which states that LF-copying is allowed only when the copied element does not enter φ-agreement.

Following Chomsky's (2000, 2008) assumption that φ-agreement requires an unvalued Case feature on the goal nominal in (18), Saito (2007) claims that LF-copying is blocked in English by Agree in the probe-goal mechanism of Chomsky (2000).

(18) Activation Condition (**AC**):
      The goal nominal must have [uCase] to undergo φ-agreement with the probe head.

(adapted from Chomsky 2000: 123)

In languages with φ-agreement, the copied nominal has already had its Case feature valued; hence, the copying operation leaves [uφ] unvalued on its agree-mate. An English example from Saito (2007) is provided in (19). AC blocks copying of the already-case-valued DP, *his friend*, to the ellipsis site in (19d). Thus, the predicate cannot enter φ-agreement with any DP. Consequently, its unvalued φ-features remain unvalued. Such problems do not arise in Japanese, as it lacks φ-agreement.

(19) a.   John brought [$_{DP}$ his friend].

  b.   *But Bill did not bring [e].

  c.   John [$v_{[u\varphi]}$]   brought [his friend$_{[v\varphi,\ uCase]}$]]

  d.   *...Bill did not [$v_{[u\varphi]}$] bring   [his friend$_{[v\varphi,\ ACC]}$]]

*φ-agreement (no [uCase] on the goal)

(adapted from Saito 2007: 215)

Although AAH seems successful, there is a technical problem.[14] To al-low AC to rule out the possibility of LF-copying and AE in English, the copy-ing operation of *his friend* must occur in narrow syntax before Transfer, as Saito's account relies on Agree, which is a formal operation in narrow syntax. However, such an LF-copying operation can only be accomplished in LF after Transfer, which raises a technical problem with Saito's AAH. Therefore, Saito's (2007) analysis is incompatible with the present study.

1.7.   Summary and the Organization of the Book

I argued that it is reasonable that lexical categories are invariant across lan-guages, while functional categories are subject to variation, as only the former serve as the primary ingredients in the design of human language as an instru-ment of thought. Furthermore, I argued that it is natural to assume variation in the presence / absence of agreement features across languages, as the fea-tures are of functional categories and subject to variation. I argued that the statement in (20) can be made (Fukui 1990, 2013, Chomsky 2015a):

(20)   **The Agreement Parametrization Hypothesis:** (=1)

The presence / absence of agreement features of functional catego-ries in the lexicon yields certain parametric variation.

I specifically aimed to demonstrate that Japanese lacks [uφ] in its lexicon (Fukui 1986 / 1995, 1988, Saito 2007, 2016, among many others). This book also attempts to provide several pieces of counterevidence to the EH.

I will demonstrate that certain differences between Japanese and other

---

[14] I would like to thank Takaomi Kato (p.c.) for pointing this problem out.

languages, especially English, are explained under the assumption that Japanese lacks [uφ] in its lexicon. Chapters 2 and 3 consist of case studies that support the claim that Japanese lacks [uφ]. Chapter 2 examines the problem with Chomsky's (2013) Labeling Algorithm and proposes an analysis of the labeling of several apparently unlabelable constructions in Japanese based on the assumption that Japanese lacks [uφ]. Chapter 3 provides a morphosyntactic analysis of the reasons for the absence of productive lexical VV-compounds in English and other languages with object-verb φ-agreement, based on the assumption that Japanese lacks [uφ]. In addition, I extensively discuss the licensing of Case in Japanese. Chapter 4 consists of rebuttals to previous studies that argue that Japanese has φ-agreement. Showing that none of them is persuasive enough, this chapter further supports the argument that Japanese lacks [uφ]. Chapter 5 is a summary of this book, along with a discussion of the correlation between the lack of φ-agreement and discourse orientation across languages.

Chapter 2

Labeling the Unlabelable in Japanese[1]

2.1. Introduction

This chapter presents the argument that Japanese lacks [uφ] in its lexicon based on labeling in Japanese. Chomsky (2013, 2015b) has claimed that every Syntactic Object (**SO**) must be labeled for interpretation at the interfaces, as in (1). The label is determined by applying the Labeling Algorithm (**LA**) to an SO at the timing of Transfer phase by phase. There are two ways to label such a symmetric {XP, YP} constituent, as illustrated in (2b).

(1)   All SOs that reach the interfaces must be labeled for interpretation.

(Chomsky 2013: 44)

(2)   Labeling Algorithm (LA):
       a.   In {H, XP}, LA selects the label H(ead).
       b.   In {XP, YP} …,
           (i)   movement of either XP or YP enables the lower copy to be invisible from LA, and the structure is labeled as the visible H(ead), X or Y; or
          (ii)   the structure is labeled by the most prominent shared fea-

---

[1] This chapter is a radically revised and extended version of Kobayashi (2018a).

21

ture F on X and Y as <F, F>.

(adapted from Chomsky 2013: 46)

In (3), the label of $\alpha = \{DP, vP\}$ is determined because the DP internally merges with TP, rendering the lower copy invisible from LA, as in (2bi); hence, α is unambiguously labeled as vP. Another {XP, YP} problem arises with the merger of DP and TP. The label of β is determined through labeling via feature-sharing in (2bii). D and T share φ-features, which undergo Agree, and β is labeled as <φ, φ>.

(3)

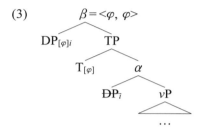

If Japanese lacks [uφ] in its lexicon, then a canonical sentence cannot be labeled via feature-sharing in (2bii) without the {XP, YP} problem with Chomsky's (2013, 2015b) original LA. This raises the question of what the labels of α and β in languages such as Japanese would look like. I propose an analysis to overcome this problem regarding labeling in a language without [uφ].[2] In this chapter, I aim to demonstrate that Japanese lacks [uφ] in its lexicon.

The remainder of this chapter is organized as follows. In Section 2.2, I first review Takita et al.'s (2016) claim that Transfer contributes to labeling (cf. Narita 2014). I then propose that the timing of Transfer is far less constrained in Japanese due to the lack of unvalued φ-features in the spirit of Fukui and Kasai (2004). Combining the two analyses, I show how the current proposal explains the labeling problems in canonical sentences, multiple subject constructions, and scrambling constructions, all of which involve {XP, YP} structures in Japanese, in Section 2.3. Section 2.4 comprises a summary of this chapter.

---

[2] See Saito (2014, 2016) and Narita and Fukui (2022) for alternative analyses.

2.2.   Timing Differences of Transfer

In this section, I propose that Japanese makes extensive use of Transfer to determine the labels of SOs due to its lack of [uφ]. The analysis incorporates the insight of Fukui and Kasai (2004) that the absence of uninterpretable features in Japanese makes the timing and domain of Spell-Out more flexible than in English. Following Takita et al.'s (2016) claim that Spell-Out contributes to determining the labels of SOs, I propose a novel analysis of why multiple subject constructions and scrambling are possible in Japanese in light of labeling (Chomsky 2013).

2.2.1.   Labeling via Transfer (Narita 2014, Takita et al. 2016)

Let us briefly review Takita et al.'s (2016) argument below. They claim that Transfer (or Spell-Out, in their terms) determines the label of an otherwise unlabelable structure. In (4), the label of the embedded clause α is not determined by LA since <which book> and C$_{[-Q]}$ do not share [+Q] or [−Q] features. Takita et al. (2016) suggest that Transfer applies to TP, which enables LA to detect C$_{[-Q]}$ as the label of α, as presented in (5).

(4)   a.   I wonder [$_\alpha$ which book Bob thinks John bought].
      b.   [$_\alpha$ <which book> [$_{XP}$ C$_{[-Q]}$ [$_{TP}$ …]]]

(5)   a.

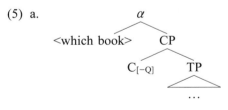

      b.

(adapted from Takita et al. 2016: 185)

What Transfer does in (5) is that it makes TP invisible from Search in {C, TP} (cf. Shim and Epstein 2015). Following Narita (2014), Takita et al. (2016) assume that a head in an SO becomes a candidate of the label again when the complement is transferred. This is compatible with Chomsky's (2012: 66) assumption that a singleton set is equivalent to its member in syntax in (6).[3]

(6) $\{X\} = X$

Since Transfer "recycles" phasal C in CP as a lexical item again in (5), LA correctly determines the label of $\{\{$which book$\}$, C$\}$ as C. This is the essence of their analysis that Transfer contributes to labeling an SO.[4]

The working hypothesis is that the complement of a phasal head will be deactivated from the active workspace of narrow syntax (Chomsky 2008: 143). One may wonder whether such "recycling" in (5) violates some strengthened versions of the No Tampering Condition (Chomsky 2008), presented in (7).

(7)   Merge of α and β leaves the two SOs unchanged.

(Chomsky 2008: 138)

Narita (2014: 78) emphasizes that Transfer does not modify the structure itself, but simply makes the phase head visible for further computation in narrow syntax. Following Narita (2014), I assume that a phasal head retains its function after Transfer in narrow syntax, as Search detects a singleton set equivalent to its member lexical item, as presented in (6).

2.2.2.   On the Timing of Transfer (Fukui and Kasai 2004)

To the best of my knowledge, Fukui and Sakai (2003) and Fukui and Kasai (2004) were the first to associate the absence of uninterpretable features and the timing of Spell-Out in Japanese. Specifically, they attempt to reduce the optionality of scrambling in Japanese to the free application of Spell-Out. Chomsky (1995) suggests that Spell-Out may apply at any point through the derivation, but the existence of uninterpretable features restricts the range of

---

[3] Naoki Fukui (p.c.) points out that this is mathematically incorrect, as $\{\emptyset\}$ is not equivalent to its member $\emptyset$. However, I follow Chomsky (2012) and assume that a singleton set is equivalent to its member as far as syntactic structure is concerned (Nagamori 2020: 16).

[4] Chomsky et al. (2019) claim that Transfer (TRANSFER) does not eliminate structure from the workspace but only makes the transferred domain inaccessible to subsequent manipulation (Chomsky et al. 2019: 241).

timing (Fukui and Kasai 2004).   Based on this, Fukui and Kasai (2004) claim that Spell-Out can apply far more freely in Japanese than in English, since the lack of uninterpretable features poses no constraint on the timing of the application of Spell-Out.

Assuming like Chomsky (2000, 2001) that vP and CP are phases, Fukui and Kasai (2004: 116) further propose that nominal phrases are also phases. Spell-Out in Fukui and Kasai (2004) was adopted from Chomsky (2001), which allows the entire phase, including the phasal head, to be sent to the PF. To derive the object-subject order in (8), they propose that sections spelled-out earlier precedes the others in linear order.[5]

(8) Piza-o$_i$ Taro-ga e_i tabe-ta   (koto).
    pizza-ACC Taro-NOM   eat-PAST fact
    '(That) Taro ate pizza.'

(Fukui and Kasai 2004: 116)

The object NP in (8), *piza-o* 'pizza' is spelled-out independently in (9), followed by another application of Spell-Out at the CP level in (10).   It derives the object-subject order, or more precisely, the object-CP order in PF.

(9)   VP

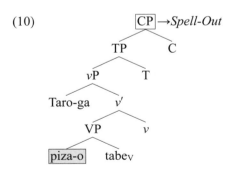

    piza-o   tabe$_V$
    ↓*Spell-Out*

(Fukui and Kasai 2004: 116)

(10)   CP →*Spell-Out*

             TP   C

          vP   T

     Taro-ga v'

       VP v

     piza-o tabe$_V$

(*ibid*)

---

[5] Note that the current proposal does not necessarily follow their assumption of how spelled-out objects are linearized.

Although their assumptions might be incompatible with the current theory of labeling, I follow Fukui and Kasai's (2004) insightful proposal regarding the timing of Spell-Out, which states that the timing of Transfer is not restricted by unvalued φ-features in Japanese, as it lacks them. Below, I combine the labeling via Transfer (Takita et al. 2016) and the insight of Fukui and Kasai (2004) and propose that Japanese makes extensive use of labeling via Transfer since the timing of Transfer is far less restricted than in English due to its lack of [uφ].[6]

2.2.3. Proposal

I propose that the timing of Transfer is systematically conditioned by the presence / absence of [uφ]. As Richards (2007) indicates, valuation of the uninterpretable features and Transfer must apply simultaneously; otherwise, they would become indistinguishable from the inherently valued features. Chomsky (2015b), among others, claims that memory regarding syntactic derivations is phase-based. I assume that memory of syntactic derivation is based on the Transfer domain. In other words, derivational memory is maintained only in the single transferred domain; hence, the inherently and derivationally valued features can be distinguished only if they are transferred simultaneously.

This book focuses on φ-features. The abovementioned Richards's (2007) problem does not arise concerning φ-features in Japanese, as its lexicon lacks [uφ]. Here, I assume that Transfer can, in principle, apply at any point in

---

[6] Regarding Case in Japanese, I argue that it is licensed with no recourse to φ-agreement. In this book, I follow Zushi's (2014, 2016) analysis of Case valuation via merger. Her original Case valuation rules presume that Case is valued when a nominal phrase merges with a head (lexical or phasal). I slightly modify Zushi's rules below. How Case is licensed in Japanese is discussed in Chapter 3.

   (i) The revised Case valuation rules in Japanese:
- a. When a nominal phrase becomes the sister of V, its Case feature is valued as accusative.
- b. When a nominal phrase becomes the sister of *v* or *n*, its Case feature is valued as nominative or genitive.
- c. Otherwise (i.e., when a nominal phrase becomes the sister of other heads), the Case feature of a nominal phrase is valued as dative.

(cf. Zushi 2016)

derivation, but it must apply when [uφ] is valued; otherwise, the problem pointed out by Richards (2007) arises. Although the timing of Transfer itself is free, [uφ] in English leads derivations to crash at the interfaces unless Transfer applies simultaneously with the feature valuation.[7] On the other hand, Transfer may apply at any point in the derivation in Japanese, as demonstrated in (11).[8] Therefore, it follows that in Japanese, the timing of Transfer is not restricted by the timing of φ-feature valuation.

(11) **Proposal**: The timing differences of Transfer in Japanese and in English

    a. Japanese: Transfer *may* apply at any point, due to its lack of [uφ].

    b. English: Transfer *must* apply at the valuation of [uφ].

2.3.   Consequences

I argue that the current analysis, which is based on the assumption that Japanese lacks [uφ], resolves the labeling problem of {XP, YP} structures in Japanese. First, I demonstrate how the {XP, YP} problem between External Argument (**EA**) and vP is solved in simple transitive sentences in Japanese. Thereafter, we observe that the proposal in (11) accurately captures why multiple subject constructions in (12) and scrambling in (13) are available in Japanese. Both create {XP, YP} structures, as schematically illustrated in (14).

(12) Harvard-ga   seisuuron-ga   daigakuinsei-ga
        Harvard-NOM number.theory-NOM grad.students-NOM
        sono-gakkai-ni   ki-ta.
        that-conference-to come-PAST

---

[7] I continue to assume that [uF] violates the Principle of Full Interpretation at the interfaces, contrary to Preminger (2014).

[8] I assume that Japanese has [uCase] though it lacks [uφ] in the lexicon. For Case valuation in Japanese, see Chapter 3 for details. I claim that Richards's problem does not occur when [uCase] is valued in Japanese, since there is no corresponding [vCase] in the lexicon. Therefore, there is no need to distinguish derivationally valued features from inherently valued features as for Case features.

'As for Harvard, the graduate students of the number theory came to the conference.'

(adapted from Fukui 2011: 89)

(13) a.   Taro-ga   Ziro-ni   Hanako-o   shookaisi-ta.
          Taro-NOM Ziro-DAT Hanako-ACC introduce-PAST
          'Taro introduced Hanako to Ziro.'

    b.   Hanako-o$_i$ Taro-ga   Ziro-ni t_i shookaisi-ta.

(14) a.   [$_\alpha$ NP$_1$-ga, [$_\beta$ NP$_2$-ga, [$_\gamma$ NP$_3$-ga, …[$_{vP}$…v]…]]]

α, β, and γ = {XP, YP}

    b.   [$_\alpha$ NP-o$_i$, [$_\beta$ NP-ga […~~NP-o$_i$~~…]]] α and β = {XP, YP}

2.3.1.   Labeling of a Canonical Sentence in Japanese

Let us examine how a sentence with a transitive verb is derived in Japanese under the proposal in (11). First, the Internal Argument (**IA**) and V merge to create a set in (15a), which is followed by the merger of v in (15b). The EA is introduced in (15c), and Transfer applies to the complement of v. The Transfer in (15c) makes VP invisible from Search; hence, what is accessible to Search is {EA, {v}} (= {EA, v}), which is labeled as vP.

(15) a.

b.

c.

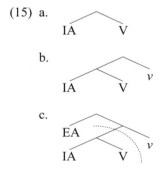

Label({EA, {{IA, V}, v}}) = vP

I assume with Fukui (1986 / 1995) and many others that the subject in Japanese does not raise to the T-domain. After C and T are introduced, the SOs are labeled as TP and CP, respectively in (16).

(16)
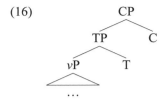

2.3.2.   Labeling of Multiple Subject Constructions

The proposal in (11) correctly explains why the multiple subject constructions are possible in Japanese (cf. Fujita 2010). Since Merge is free (Chomsky 2004), multiple nominals may externally merge with the edge of the structure, as in (17).

(17)   Merger:

   a.
   NP_1 VP v

   b.
   NP_2 NP_1 VP v

   c.
   NP_3 NP_2 NP_1 VP v

After the Transfer of VP in (18a), Search can only see v in $\{VP, v\}$. A singleton set is identical to its member; thus, $\{v\} = v$ (Chomsky 2012: 66 and Takita et al. 2016). At this point, Search views NP_1 as the closest complement of v in $\{NP_1, \{VP, v\}\}$ since VP is no longer visible. I assume that Transfer of NP_1 may apply, as Search detects $\{NP_1, v\}$ in $\{NP_1, \{VP, v\}\}$ (i.e., $\{NP_1, \{VP, v\}\} = \{NP_1, \{v\}\} = \{NP_1, v\}$). Transfer then applies to NP_1 in (18b), which results in $\{NP_1, \{VP, v\}\}$, rendering NP_1 invisible from Search. The same is true for NP_2. If Transfer does not further apply in (18d), then $\{NP_3, \{NP_2, \{NP_1, \{VP, v\}\}\}\}$ is labeled as vP when transferred.

(18)   Transfer:

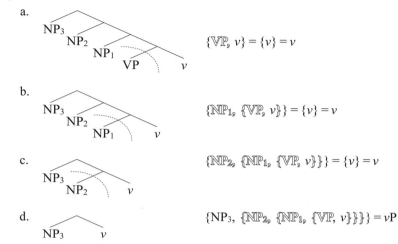

a. $\{\text{VP}, v\} = \{v\} = v$

b. $\{\text{NP}_1, \{\text{VP}, v\}\} = \{v\} = v$

c. $\{\text{NP}_2, \{\text{NP}_1, \{\text{VP}, v\}\}\} = \{v\} = v$

d. $\{\text{NP}_3, \{\text{NP}_2, \{\text{NP}_1, \{\text{VP}, v\}\}\}\} = v\text{P}$

The proposed mechanism predicts that multiple nominative constructions are available in Japanese. I assume that nominative Case is valued when a nominal becomes the sister of v (cf. Zushi 2014, 2016). As multiple nominals derivationally become sisters of v in (18), each nominal receives nominative Case. Note that the multiple genitive construction can be derived via the same mechanism if we replace V and v with N and n.[9] The analysis captures

---

[9] A typical example of multiple genitive constructions is presented in (i) below:

(i)   MIT-de-no   senshuu-no   Chomsky-no   so-no   koogi
      MIT-at-GEN last.week-GEN Chomsky-GEN that-GEN lecture
      Lit. 'MIT's last week's Chomsky's that lecture'

(Fukui 1988: 257)

I claim that nominative Case is valued when a nominal derivationally becomes the sister of v, while genitive Case is valued when a nominal becomes the sister of n. The Case valuation rules adopted in this book are as follows:

(ii)   Case valuation rules to be discussed in Chapter 3:
   a.   When a nominal phrase becomes the sister of V, its Case feature is valued as accusative.
   b.   When a nominal phrase becomes the sister of v or n, its Case feature is valued as nominative or genitive.
   c.   Otherwise (i.e., when a nominal phrase becomes the sister of other heads), the Case feature of a nominal phrase is valued as dative.

(cf. Zushi 2016)

Fukui's insight that the unbounded merge is in full force in Japanese (Fukui 2011: 90).

Some may wonder what happens when NP_1 is transferred after the VP is transferred in English. Transfer itself is applicable. However, since NP_1 is not convergent due to the existence of [uCase] on nominals, such application of Transfer at this point does not satisfy Full Interpretation at the interfaces. In summary, this section has provided a multiple-Transfer analysis of the labeling of multiple subject constructions in Japanese. The labels of each node are determined via LA (Minimal Search) when Transfer applies (Chomsky 2013, 2015b). The analysis predicts that α, β, and γ in $\{_\alpha NP_3, \{_\beta NP_2, \{_\gamma NP_1, \{VP, v\}\}\}\}$ (irrelevant details are omitted) are all interpreted as vP at the interfaces without any {XP, YP} problems.[10]

2.3.3. Labeling of Scrambling Constructions

A further consequence of the proposal in (11) concerns the labeling of scrambling constructions in (19). The proposal in this chapter explains how the {XP, YP} structures created by scrambling are labeled based on the assumption that Japanese lacks [uφ].

(19) a.　Taro-ga　Hanako-o　home-ta.
　　　　Taro-NOM Hanako-ACC praise-PAST
　　　　'Taro praised Hanako.'
　　b.　Hanako-o$_i$　Taro-ga　t_i　home-ta.

Let us observe the derivation of (19) in (20). In (20a), the IA internally merges with the edge of the structure. If Transfer of {IA, V} applies, the structure will be like (20b). Subsequently, Transfer of the EA applies in (20c). If Transfer does not apply further, the label of the SO will be vP since Search unambiguously detects v in (20d).

---

[10] One may question as to whether the multiple accusative construction is available in this mechanism. The analysis predicts that multiple accusative assignment is generally unavailable, as V is not a phasal head and so it cannot (multiply) Transfer its complement. This is compatible with the general ban on multiple occurrences of accusative -o marked nominals in Japanese (Harada 1973, Shibatani 1978a, cf. Kuroda 1988).

(20) a.

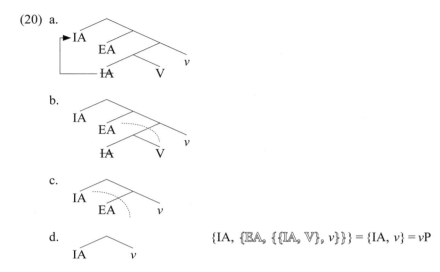

b.

c.

d. $\{$IA, $\{$EA, $\{\{$IA, V$\}$, $v\}\}\}$ = $\{$IA, $v\}$ = vP

A simple case of scrambling does not pose any problem following the proposal in (11) that the timing of Transfer is not restricted in Japanese.[11] Scrambling in Japanese is not limited to clause-internal ones. The proposal in (11) predicts that {XP, YP} structures created by long-distance scrambling are also labelable. The data dealt with here are sentences like (21).

(21) Ringo-o$_i$ Taro-ga   [Hanako-ga t_i tabe-ta   to] omow-ta.
      apple-ACC Taro-NOM Hanako-NOM   eat-PAST that think-PAST
      'Taro thought that Hanako ate an apple.'

Let us examine the derivation of such long-distance scrambling step-by-step. The tree-diagrammatic representations are given in (22) through (25). After v

---

[11] The analysis predicts that scrambling to TP results in labeling failure since T is not a phase head. One may then consider whether it is compatible with the assumption that some scrambling targets TP (or IP) in Japanese. The only evidence for the scrambling to TP comes from the mixed A / A'-property of sentence-internal scrambling. It has been observed that sentence-internal scrambling shows somewhat mixed properties of A / A'-movement in the literature (Saito 1992, 2003, and Tada 1993, among others). Nemoto (1999) notes that Saito (1989) suggests that such scrambling targets the adjoined position of IP. Under the current analysis, when scrambling shows A-property, then it is scrambling to vP. On the other hand, when it exhibits some A'-property, its landing site is CP. In summary, although the current analysis does not allow scrambling to TP, it is compatible with the peculiar property of middle-distance scrambling.

has completed its argument structure in (22a), IA raises up to the edge of the
structure, as in (22b). Transfer of {*ringo*, V} applies in (22c). Then, T and
C are introduced into the derivation, as illustrated in (22d).

(22) a.

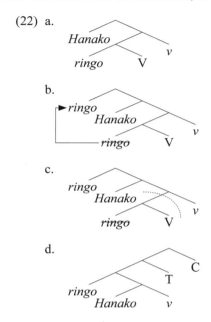

Subsequently, IA (*ringo*) raises up to the edge of the embedded clause in
(23a). Next, Transfer of TP applies, as in (23b). Thus, α is labeled as *v*P.

(23) a.

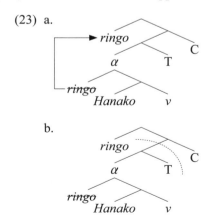

In (24a), the matrix verb *omow-* 'think' and *v* together with its subject *Taro* are introduced via external Merge. Another internal Merge applies to the scrambled IA (*ringo*) in (24b). Transfer then applies to the complement of *v*, as presented in (24c).

(24) a.

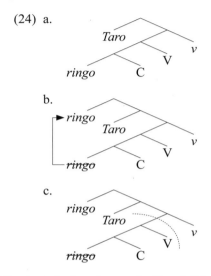

b.

c.

After introducing the matrix T and C in (25a), *ringo* undergoes internal Merge to the edge of the structure. Subsequently, the complement of C is transferred, as in (25b). The label of β is determined as *v*P, as *ringo* is an invisible lower copy. Thanks to multiple applications of Transfer, γ and δ are labeled as TP and CP respectively when LA (or Minimal Search) applies to them.

(25) a.

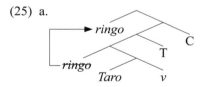

b.

$\delta = \mathrm{CP}$

$\gamma = \mathrm{TP}$

$\beta = v\mathrm{P}$

The current proposal does not predict that scrambling is also possible in English. Since a DP bears [uCase], it must be valued before Transfer.[12] I assume with Chomsky (2000, 2008), among others, that Case is valued as a reflex of φ-agreement in English. The IA in English receives the accusative Case via φ-agreement with V. After scrambling of the IA, φ-agreement cannot occur, as the goal IA is no longer c-commanded by the probe. The [uCase] on the IA remains unvalued; therefore, the derivation crashes at the interfaces. The problem does not arise in Japanese, as [uCase] is valued via sister relations created by Merge in Japanese (Zushi 2014, 2016, Nagamori 2020). I argue that the IA receives the accusative Case when it becomes a sister with V in the base-generated position. Therefore, the IA can undergo scrambling in Japanese. See Chapter 3 for an extensive discussions of Case valuation in Japanese based on Zushi's (2014, 2016) Case valuation rules via merger.

One may question whether the analysis is compatible with A'-movement, such as topicalization and *wh*-movement in English, as in (26) and (27). These data are perfectly grammatical in English.

(26) a.   That book$_i$, John bought t_i.

b.   That book$_i$, Mary thinks that John bought t_i.

---

[12] The current proposal predicts that multiple scrambled PPs do not cause labeling failure in English, which can be problematic. Multiple scrambling (topicalization) of PPs is prohibited in English, as in (i).

(i) a.   Bill sent a present to John for Mary.
   b. *To John, for Mary, Bill sent a present.
   c. *For Mary, to John, Bill sent a present.

How PPs in English receive labels is left unresolved in Chomsky's (2013, 2015b) LA. I leave this issue for future research.

(27) a.   Who$_i$ did you see t_i?
      b.   What$_i$ did you think that Mary bought t_i?

I assume that the objects enter Agree with V simultaneously with an internal merger to the edge of vP at the phase level (cf. Chomsky 2007b, 2008). This option is only available with elements with features related to A′-movement, such as Q-related and Topic/Focus features. I speculate on a reason to underpin this exceptional assumption: only operators with Q-related features and elements with Topic/Focus features can undergo internal merge simultaneously with Transfer and [uφ] valuation. If this option is not available, the derivation will crash due to the existence of unvalued features that should be valued later in the C-domain. The above option (i.e., simultaneous valuation, Transfer, and internal merger) cannot be applied to canonical arguments, as they do not bear any features regarding A′-movement that must be valued through Agree with the C head later in the derivation.

2.4. Summary

In this chapter, I proposed that the absence of [uφ] in Japanese allows it to apply Transfer in a far less restricted form in its timing (Fukui and Kasai 2004), as in (28) (=11). Following the insight of Fukui and Kasai (2004) and the idea of Narita (2014), Takita et al. (2016) and others that Transfer contributes to labeling, I have demonstrated that the proposal in (28) successfully provides explanations for the labeling of {XP, YP} structures created in (i) canonical sentences, (ii) multiple subject constructions, and (iii) scrambling constructions in Japanese.

(28) **Proposal**: The timing differences of Transfer in Japanese and English
      a.   Japanese: Transfer *may* apply at any point, due to its lack of [uφ].
      b.   English: Transfer *must* apply at the valuation of [uφ].

Chomsky's (2013, 2015b) LA cannot label canonical sentences or several other constructions in Japanese based on the assumption that it lacks [uφ] in the lexicon. I proposed a syntactic analysis to overcome the {XP, YP} problems that Chomsky's LA faces in labeling in a language without φ-agreement (see Saito 2014, 2016, and Narita and Fukui 2022 and for different approaches to this problem). If the proposed analysis is on the right track, it lends credence to the claim that Japanese lacks [uφ] and the presence/absence of agreement features yields certain linguistic variations. In summary, the case study in this chapter supports the proposal of this book.[13]

---

[13] See Kobayashi (2021) for an analysis of how the proposal in (11) works in the C-domain.

Chapter 3

φ-agreement and Lexical VV-compounds[1]

3.1. Introduction

In this chapter, I highlight a correlation between the absence of productive lexical VV-compounds and the presence of object-verb φ-agreement from a comparative perspective. Thereafter, I propose how the derivation of lexical VV-compounds is blocked in languages with object-verb φ-agreement. Following this, I discuss how Case is valued in Japanese. This chapter provides further support for the claim that Japanese lacks [uφ] in its lexicon.

The definition of lexical VV-compounds in this chapter is presented in (1), cited from Kageyama (2016). The non-interruptibility principle of lexical integrity states that the internal structure of compounds must not be affected by syntactic operations such as movement (Anderson 1992). The point is that multiple Vs behave as structurally adjacent indivisible units in lexical VV-compounds. Based on (1), I propose an exploratory generalization regarding lexical VV-compounds and object-verb φ-agreement, as presented in (2).

(1) **A definition of lexical VV-compounds:**
     Lexical VV-compounds are endocentric VV-compounds that satisfy

---

[1] This chapter is a radically revised and extended version of Kobayashi (2018b).

the non-interruptibility principle of lexical integrity and behave as structurally adjacent indivisible V^0 units.

(adapted from Kageyama 2016: 278)

(2) **An exploratory generalization:**
     If a language has object-verb φ-agreement, then it cannot have productive lexical VV-compounds.

VV-compounds in Japanese are divided into two groups: lexical and syntactic VV-compounds. It has long been assumed that the lexical VV-compounds are created in the lexicon, whereas syntactic VV-compounds are derived in syntax, as their names indicate (Kageyama 1993). Japanese abounds in lexical VV-compounds, as demonstrated in (3) (Fukushima 2005), in which the second heads are neither functional nor auxiliarized unlike syntactic compounds presented in (4). I focus on such lexical VV-compounds in this book.

(3) Examples of lexical VV-compounds in Japanese:
   a. tobi-ori
       jump-drop
       'jump off'
   b. nomi-aruk
       drink-walk
       'go barhopping'
   c. naguri-koros
       hit-kill
       'beat to death'
   d. tare-nagas
       drip-pour
       'drain'
   e. koroge-oti
       roll-fall
       'roll down'

(4) Examples of syntactic VV-compounds in Japanese:
   a. aisi-tuduke
       love-ASP$_{continue}$

b.   utai-hazime
    sing-ASP$_{begin}$

c.   kaki-oe
    write-ASP$_{finish}$

d.   tabe-sase
    eat-CAUS

e.   home-rare
    praise-PASS

(Kageyama 1993)

Whether lexical VV-compounds are derived in the lexicon or in syntax is controversial (Kageyama 1993, Nishiyama 2008). In this chapter, I follow Nishiyama (2008) and Nishiyama and Ogawa (2014), among many others, in assuming that they are derived in syntax. Although the term *lexical* in lexical VV-compounds is confusing, I will continue to use it to refer to the VV-compounds listed in (3), which are the foci of this chapter. A type of VV-compounds that we do not explore here satisfies the two well-known diagnostics of syntactic VV-compounds in (5). In (5a), the first verb of syntactic VV-compounds can be substituted by *soo su-* 'do so'. Likewise, in (5b), the first verb of only syntactic VV-compounds can be passivized by *-(r)are* 'PASS'.

(5)   Syntactic criteria for the distinction between lexical and syntactic VV-compounds:

  a.   *Soo su*-substitution:

	Lexical:	tobi-ori	→	*soo	si-ori
		jump-fall		so	do-fall
		nomi-aruk	→	*soo	si-aruk
		drink-walk		so	do-walk
	Syntactic:	aisi-tsuzuke	→	soo	si-tsuzuke
		love-ASP$_{continue}$		so	do-ASP$_{continue}$
		utai-hazime	→	soo	si-hazime
		sing-ASP$_{begin}$		so	do-ASP$_{begin}$

  b.   Passivization of V1:

	Lexical:	naki-haras	→	*nak-are-haras
		cry-swell		cry-PASS-swell
		naguri-koros	→	*nagu-rare-koros
		punch-kill		punch-PASS-kill

Syntactic: kaki-owar   →   kak-are-owar

write-ASP$_{finish}$ write-PASS-ASP$_{finish}$

tabe-sase   →   tabe-rare-sase

eat-CAUS   eat-PASS-CAUS

(adapted from Kageyama 2016: 278)

The second element in syntactic VV-compounds is analyzed either as a functional head or as an auxiliarized element without the status of lexical categories (Yashima 2008, Fukuda 2012). Since they show quite different behaviors from lexical VV-compounds and are usually assumed to be derived from biclausal structures (plus possibly restructuring), I do not discuss these syntactic VV-compounds in this book.

The aim of this chapter is twofold: I demonstrate that only languages without object-verb φ-agreement can have productive lexical VV-compounds. Then, I propose a morphosyntactic analysis of how productive lexical VV-compounds are blocked in languages with object-verb φ-agreement. Section 3.2 presents lexical VV-compounds in languages without object-verb φ-agreement. Section 3.3 investigates two languages with overt object-verb φ-agreement. Following this, I propose an exploratory generalization regarding the presence of productive lexical VV-compounds and the absence of object-verb φ-agreement in languages. Section 3.4 provides a morphosyntactic analysis that blocks productive lexical VV-compounds in languages with object-verb φ-agreement. Section 3.5 presents an extensive discussion on how Case is valued in Japanese. Section 3.6 comprises a summary of this chapter.

3.2.   VV-compounds in Languages without Object φ-agreement

I first observe data from Japanese, Korean, Mongolian, Malayalam, Turkish, and Bangla. They all lack object-verb φ-agreement. Japanese, Korean, Mongolian, and Malayalam lack φ-agreement altogether, while Turkish and Bangla only have subject-predicate φ-agreement and lack object-verb φ-agreement. The canonical sentences showing that they all lack object-verb φ-agreement are illustrated in (6) through (10).

(6)   Korean:
      John-i   Mary / Nay / Ai-lul   kkwulh-e anc-hi-ess-ta.
      John-NOM   Mary / I / children-ACC   kneel-LK   sit-CAUS-PAST-DECL
      'John made Mary / I / children kneel down.'

                                    (adapted from Ko and Sohn 2015)

(7)   Mongolian:
      Bat-Ø   nama-ig / chama-ig / ter-ig / bid-nig / tanar-ig / ted-nig
      Bat-NOM   me / you / him / us / you / them-ACC
      har-san.
      see-PERF
      'Bat saw me / you / him / us / you / them.'

                                            (Sakamoto 2011: 33)

(8)   Malayalam:
      Siita eni / namu / niŋŋal / raaman-e sneehikkunnnu.
      Sita   I / we / you / Raman-ACC   love
      'Sita loves me / us / you / Raman.'

                                    (adapted from Jayaseelan 1999: 30–44)

(9)   Turkish:
      Can üç   hırsız / ben / biz yakala-dı.
      John three burglar / I / we   catch-PAST.3SG
      'John caught three burglars / me / us.'

                                    (adapted from Şener and Takahashi 2010: 88)

(10) Bangla:
      Ami æk-ṭa / du-To / tin-Ta   boi / tumi dekhechi.
      1.SG one-CL / two-CL / three-CL book / you seen-1.SG
      'I have seen one / two / three book(s) / you.'

                                    (adapted from Bhattacharya 1999: 12)

In addition to Japanese, productive lexical VV-compounds are attested in all
these languages, including Korean, Mongolian, Malayalam, Turkish, and
Bangla, as illustrated in (11) through (15).

(11)   Korean:
    a.   ara-tut
        know-hear
        'understand'
    b.   kulm-tɕuri
        hunger-starve
        'starve'

                        (Paschen 2014)

(12)   Mongolian:
    a.   dza:j-ögöx
        teach-give
        'show'
    b.   avc-irex
        take-bring
        'bring'

                        (Khurelbat 1992)

(13)   Malayalam:
    a.   pookuwaan-anuwadicc
        go-permit
        'permit leave'
    b.   ār-āy
        become.full-search
        'investigate'

                        (Krishnamurti 2003)

(14)   Turkish:
    a.   gelince-şaşır
        come-surprise
        'come to surprise'
    b.   geçip-git
        pass-go
        'leave through'

                        (Kuribayashi 2006)

(15)   Bangla:
    a. uRe-gE
        fly-go
        'fly away'
    b. ghumiye-poR
        sleep-fall
        'fall asleep'

(Paul 2003)

In the next section, I examine two languages with overt object-verb φ-agreement.

3.3.   The Lack of Lexical VV-compounds in Languages with Object φ-agreement

This section focuses on two languages: Welsh and Swahili. These languages do not allow any combination of endocentric verb-verb compounds. In these languages, the object undergoes overt φ-agreement with the verb, as illustrated in (16) and (17).

(16)   Welsh:
    Mae   Steffan yn   dy   garu   di.
    be.PRES.3.SG Steffan PROG 2.SG love.INF you.2SG
    'Steffan loves you.'

(Borsley et al. 2007: 27)

(17)   Swahili:
    Juma a-li-mw-u-a   fisi.
    Juma 1.sg-past-3.sg-kill hyena
    'Juma killed a hyena.'

(adapted from Vitale 1981: 17)

    Based on the observations in the two types of languages, (i) Japanese, Korean, Mongolian, Malayalam, Turkish, and Bangla, and (ii) Welsh and Swahili, I propose an exploratory generalization regarding the presence of lexical VV-compounds and the absence of the object-verb φ-agreement, as in (18).

(18)   **An exploratory generalization:** (=2)

If a language has object-verb φ-agreement, then it cannot have productive lexical VV-compounds.

3.4.   Blocking of Lexical VV-compounds by φ-features

To formalize the descriptive generalization in (18), I propose a morphosyntactic analysis that blocks the derivation of lexical VV-compounds in languages
with object-verb φ-agreement. As for the structure of lexical VV-compounds,
I follow a slightly modified version of the structure in Nishiyama (1998,
2008) and Nishiyama and Ogawa (2014), in which they are base-generated via
direct merger.

Why is VV-compounding blocked in languages with object-verb
φ-agreement? Recall that the verbal stems of VV-compounds must, by definition, be adjacent to each other in languages with productive lexical VV-
compounds. In languages with φ-features, I concur with Harbour (2016),
among others, that φ-nodes exist adjacent to the verbal stems at the syntax-
morphology interface. φ-nodes are proposed as the locus of φ-inflection such
as number morphology (Thornton 2019, among others). The derivation of
lexical VV-compounds in languages with φ-features proceeds as follows.
First, Vs inherit φ-features from v via feature inheritance (Chomsky 2008).
After Transfer, φ-features realize as φ-nodes, which are adjacent to verbal
stems. As a result, a φ-node on the first V intervenes between the verbal
stems, which breaks the structural adjacency of the verbal stems. Even if one
assumes that the φ-node on the stem precedes the corresponding stem, the
φ-node on the second stem intervenes between the two verbal stems. The
structure in which a φ-node follows the corresponding verbal stem is illustrated in (19).

(19)

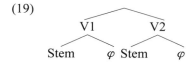

Languages with object-verb φ-agreement cannot form productive lexical VV-
compounds because the following two requirements contradict each other:

(20) a.   Two verbal stems must be adjacent to each other; and

b.   φ-nodes must attach to the verbal stems.

The structure results in the contradiction of two requirements (20a) and (20b) at the syntax-morphology interface after Transfer. Therefore, languages with object-verb φ-agreement lacks productive lexical VV-compounds.

If only the second V in VV-compounds inherits [uφ] from *v*, then the above problem does not occur. I argue that the derivation crashes even under the assumption that only one of the Vs undergoes feature inheritance. Note that [uφ] on V cannot probe into the internal argument, which is not c-commanded by either the first or second V. Therefore, φ-feature agreement fails and the derivation crashes at the interfaces.[2]

One may wonder if the *v*-to-V φ-feature inheritance is necessary. Let us briefly review Richards's (2007) argument here. Assuming that phase heads are the locus of unvalued features, Richards (2007) claims that a non-phase head must inherit features from a phase head, based on two assumptions, presented in (21a) and (21b).

(21) a.   Transfer must occur as soon as valuation occurs.

b.   The edge of a phase is transferred separately from the phasal complement.

If unvalued features remain on the phase head, they cause a problem. Derivationally valued features must be transferred upon valuation, since the interfaces cannot distinguish them from inherently valued features, as memory is based on the Transfer domain (see Chapter 2). If unvalued features receive values on the phase head, then they are not transferred due to (21b). Therefore, I conclude with Richards (2007) that feature inheritance must occur.[3, 4]

---

[2] One may wonder whether two Vs form a single V and this V inherits [uφ] from *v*. I claim that this account is problematic, as it may violate the No Tampering Condition (Chomsky 2008). Two separate Vs cannot be a single V in narrow syntax. It is not until the syntax-morphology interface that two Vs become a single V. I would like to thank Toru Ishii and Takaomi Kato (p.c.) for pointing out this issue to me.

[3] See Epstein et al. (2012) for different reasoning regarding the need of feature inheritance.

[4] As for verbs without unvalued φ-features, such as unaccusatives, I assume that they have φ-features with some values, though defective (Chomsky 2001, Fukui and Narita

3.5. Covert Object φ-agreement in English and Case Valuation in Japanese

In this section, I claim that English has covert object-verb φ-agreement. Then, I discuss Case valuation in Japanese, which lacks φ-agreement. English does not show any overt φ-morphology on verbs for the object-verb φ-agreement, as demonstrated in (22). Initially, there is no evidence of object-verb φ-agreement in English.

(22) a.   The teacher scolded John / Mary / him / her / me / you / them / us.
    b.   The student loves John / Mary / him / her / me / you / them / us.

However, I argue that the verb has φ-features and undergoes Agree with an object in English. Along the line of Chomsky (2000, 2008), I assume that Case features in languages like English and German are licensed as a reflex of φ-feature agreement.[5]   That is, the verb licenses accusative Case, entering into

---

2012 / 2017). Evidence comes from French, where participles of unaccusative verbs do show overt φ-morphology, as demonstrated in (i). If there were no φ-features on unaccusative verbs, it would be unclear why cases such as (i) show the φ-morpheme on verbs.

(i)   Hier   les   femmes   sont mortes.
      yesterday the.PL woman.PL are   dead.FEM.PL
      'The women died yesterday.'

(William Snyder p.c.)

One may wonder whether feature inheritance is necessary with unaccusatives, since their φ-features are inherently valued. I assume that valued φ-features are in the first place on unaccusative Vs in the lexicon. That inherently valued φ-features exist on lexical categories is compatible with the proposal of this book.

[5]   German is like English in that it values Case via φ-agreement. In German, expressions such as *kennen lernen* 'get to know' and *spazieren gehen* 'take a walk' exist. Initially, they seem to be the lexical VV-compounds. Neef (2009), among others, classifies them as VV-compounds. However, I argue that they are not genuine lexical VV-compounds. They are called *partikelverben*, which are *separable verbs*, as illustrated below.

(i)   Ich *lerne* keinen Mann *kennen*.
      I   learn no   man   know
      'I get to know nobody.'

(ii) *Ich *kennen-lerne* keinen Mann.

They are separated in the verb-second construction (Peter Erdmann and Haider Hubert p.c.). It violates the principle of lexical integrity in the definition of the endocentric VV-com-

φ-feature agreement with the Internal Argument (**IA**).

Although there is no direct morphological evidence of the object-verb φ-agreement in English, I maintain that there is φ-agreement between V and the IA. That IAs show pronominal Case inflections in (22) is evidence for the existence of object-verb φ-agreement in English, as Case is valued as a reflex of φ-agreement in English. Indeed, English lacks productive VV-compounds, as revealed in (23).[6]

(23)   Productive lexical VV-compounds are unavailable in English:
    a.   *jump-drop
    b.   *drink-walk
    c.   *hit-kill
    d.   *strike-smash
    e.   *drip-pour
    f.   *roll-fall

A question that arises here is how Case is licensed in languages without φ-agreement. I assume that there are two types of languages (cf. Kuroda 1988: 40), in which Case is valued via φ-agreement (Chomsky 2000, 2001) or via Merge (Zushi 2014, 2016, also see Saito 2012).

I argue that Case valuation in Japanese is not tied to φ-agreement. In this book, I follow Zushi's (2014, 2016) analysis of Case valuation via merger. Her original Case valuation rules are given in (24). Zushi's rules presume that Case is valued when a nominal phrase merges with a head.

(24)   Zushi's (2016) Case valuation rules:
    a.   When a nominal is merged with a lexical head, its case feature is valued as accusative.
    b.   When a nominal is merged with a phase head (*v* or *n*), its case feature is valued as nominative or genitive.

---

pounds. Therefore, I conclude that German lacks productive genuine lexical VV-compounds.

[6] VV-compounds in English are not productive, and certain compounds, such as *stir-fry*, *sleep-walk* and *slam-dunk*, are frozen / idiosyncratic expressions (Lieber 2005: 378). Compounds such as *drink-drive* are exocentric nominal compounds. Other apparent verb-verb compounds in English, such as *type-write* and *trickle-irrigate*, which are scarce and limited in the inventory, are analyzed as derived via morphological processes, such as back-formation from nominal compounds (i.e., *type-writer* and *trickle-irrigation*) (Yosuke Sato p.c.).

c.   Otherwise, the case feature of a nominal is valued as dative.

(Zushi 2016: 48)

I slightly modify Zushi's rules, as in (25a–c) below, so that they become compatible with the proposals in Chapter 2.[7]

(25)   The revised Case valuation rules:

a.   When a nominal phrase becomes the sister of V, its Case feature is valued as accusative.[8]

b.   When a nominal phrase becomes the sister of *v* or *n*, its Case feature is valued as nominative or genitive.

c.   Otherwise (i.e., when a nominal phrase becomes the sister of other heads), the Case feature of a nominal phrase is valued as dative.

We now explore how the Case valuation rules in (25) work. Data with canonical case patterns in Japanese that this study deals with are illustrated in (26a–d) below.

(26)   Canonical Case patterns in Japanese:

a.   Taro-***ga***   arui-ta.

Taro-NOM walk-PAST

'Taro walked.'

b.   Hanako-***ga***   ronbun-***o***   kai-ta.

Hanako-NOM paper-ACC write-PAST

'Hanako wrote a paper.'

c.   Hanako-***no***   ane

Hanako-GEN sister

'Hanako's sister'

d.   Taro-***ga***   Hanako-***ni***   okane-***o***   moraw-ta.

Taro-NOM Hanako-DAT money-ACC receive-PAST

'Taro received money from Hanako.'

---

[7]   In this book, I do not assume √ROOTS, lexical items that have no categorial information. They are assumed in the framework of Distributed Morphology (See Siddiqi 2010 and the references cited therein). In this book, I assume that lexical heads contain categorial information in the first place. N, V, A, and P create shell structures with *n*, *v*, *a*, and *p*.

[8]   I assume that a lexical VV-compound is counted as one V, a single inseparable unit; as such, when a nominal phrase becomes the sister of the lexical VV-compounds in Japanese, its Case feature is valued as accusative.

The *-ga* pattern in (26a) can be easily derived.   The subject *Taro* is merged to
the edge of *v*P, and the complement of *v* is transferred.   Thereafter, *Taro* derivationally becomes the sister of *v*, as in (27), whose Case is valued as nominative according to the rule in (25b).

(27)
     Taro   v

We move on to the *-ga -o* pattern in (26b).   The object *ronbun* 'paper'
merges with V, receiving the accusative Case value according to the rule in
(25a).   Then, *v* and the subject *Hanako* merge with the structure, as in (28a).
Thereafter, the complement of *v* is transferred, and thus *Hanako* derivationally
becomes the sister of *v* in (28b), as the complement VP becomes invisible after Transfer.   The subject *Hanako* receives the nominative Case according to
the rule in (25b).

(28) a.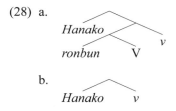
        Hanako
           ronbun   V   v

     b.
        Hanako   v

Next, we deal with the *-no* pattern in (26c).   First, N (*ane* 'elder sister')
merges with a small *n*, creating a nominal phrase.   The locus of [uCase] is *n*;
therefore, *ane* (N) does not receive genitive Case.   Next, another *n*P, *Hanako*,
merges to the structure, as in (29a).   Then, *ane* is transferred, which derivationally makes the nominal phrase *Hanako* the sister of *n*, as in (29b).
Hanako receives the genitive Case according to the rule in (25b).[9]

(29) a.
        Hanako
              ane   n

---

[9] Takaomi Kato (p.c.) pointed out that the Case valuation rules may predict that the *n*P in
{{*n*P, N}, *n*} (e.g., *tosi-no hakai* 'the city's destruction') wrongly receives dative Case, as it
is the sister of N.   The above structure presupposes that the *n*P (*tosi* 'a city') receives a
θ-role from the N (*hakai* 'destruction').   It is unclear whether the *n*P, *tosi* 'a city', receives
its θ-role from the N, *hakai* 'destruction', in the structure assumed above.   Therefore, I leave
this issue for future research.

b.

Hanako   n

Finally, we turn to the *-ga -ni -o* pattern in (26d). I assume with Zushi (2014) and Nagamori (2020) that the indirect object in the ditransitive construction is introduced with an applicative head, which is a phase head (McGinnis 2001, among others).[10] The applicative head merges with the VP, *okane-o moraw-* 'receive money'. Then, the indirect object *Hanako* merges to the edge of the structure, as in (30a). The VP is transferred, which results in (30b). According to the rule in (25c), the indirect object *Hanako* receives the dative Case. Next, *v* and the subject *Taro* are introduced via merger, as presented in (30c). Subsequently, the complement of *v* is transferred. It creates the structure in (30d), in which the subject *Taro* receives the nominative Case following the rule in (25b).

(30) a.

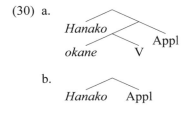

Hanako

okane   V   Appl

b.

Hanako   Appl

---

[10] In evidence from McGinnis (2002), she observes consonant mutation phenomena. Consonant mutation is blocked by the phase boundary, as in (i). In Welsh, the auxiliary *bydd* 'will.be.3sɢ' mutates to *fydd* when it becomes adjacent to *hi* 'she'. However, due to the presence of the (CP) phase boundary, the mutation is blocked.

(i)   The lack of consonant mutation across the CP phase boundary
      Dywedodd [NP hi] [CP (y) [IP bydd   hi'n   prynu car newydd]]
      said.3sɢ   she   COMP will.be.3sɢ she-PROG buy   car new
      'She said (that) she will be buying a new car.'

                                                        (Tallerman 1990: 405)

Turning now to Cibemba, a Bantu language, the applicative head also blocks consonant mutation. In this language, the causative head induces consonant mutation, as in (iia). This mutation spreads to several morphemes (McGinnis 2002). However, in the case of Root-APPL-CAUS, consonant mutation does not apply to the Root due to the existence of Appl, which creates a phase, as in (iib).

(ii) a.   *-lub-* 'be.lost' vs. *-luf-į-* 'be.lost-CAUS'
     b.   *-lub-il-* 'be.lost-APPL' vs. *-lub-is-į-* 'be.lost-APPL-CAUS' (*-luf-is-į-*)

c.

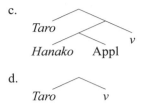

d.

Taro   *v*

Thus far, I have shown a way to value Case features in Japanese with no recourse to φ-agreement. I argued that Case in Japanese is not valued as a reflex of φ-agreement but is valued via sister relations created by merger.

3.6.   Summary

In this chapter, I highlighted a correlation between the absence of productive lexical VV-compounds and the presence of object-verb φ-agreement from a comparative perspective. Based on the observations, I proposed the generalization presented in (31).

(31)   **An exploratory generalization** (=2):

If a language has object-verb φ-agreement, then it cannot have productive lexical VV-compounds.

Following this, I proposed a morphosyntactic analysis of how lexical VV-compounds are blocked in languages with object-verb φ-agreement. Furthermore, I extensively discussed how Case is valued in Japanese with no recourse to φ-agreement. The observations that the presence of object-verb φ-agreement blocks productive lexical VV-compounds and that languages without such agreements abound in productive lexical VV-compounds support the argument that Japanese lacks [uφ] in the lexicon.

Chapter 4

Arguments against φ-agreement in Japanese

4.1. Introduction

In this chapter, I scrutinize five kinds of arguments for φ-agreement in Japanese. Although there is no conceptual necessity in unvalued φ-features, as they are LF-uninterpretable, they are often assumed even for Japanese with no overt realization. Such an assumption takes a free ride on the Strong Uniformity Thesis (**SUT**: Boeckx 2011: 210, 2014: 119, 2016: 73) in that it accepts the universal presence of [uφ]. However, SUT should not offer free rides. Rather, researchers must provide strong empirical evidence to demonstrate that SUT holds in the first place. I argue against such approaches in the study of Japanese syntax in this chapter. The five arguments for φ-agreement in Japanese that I examine in this chapter are as follows: (i) Case valuation (Ura 2000, Hiraiwa 2005, Obata 2010), (ii) nominative / genitive conversion (Hiraiwa 2001, 2005), (iii) Person restriction (Miyagawa 2010, Obata and Sugimura 2014, 2019), (iv) honorification (Toribio 1990, Ura 2000, Boeckx and Niinuma 2004), and (v) the so-called allocutive agreement (Miyagawa 2017). I offer rebuttals to each. Given that there is little evidence for φ-agreement in Japanese, the results of this chapter support the argument that Japanese lacks [uφ] in the lexicon.

4.2.   Case Valuation (Ura 2000, Hiraiwa 2005, Obata 2010)

Ura (1996, 2000) and Hiraiwa (2005), among many others, assume that Case valuation results as a reflex of φ-agreement in Japanese just as in English, along with Chomsky (2001), whose idea dates back to George and Kornfilt (1981). Recently, Obata (2010: 79) claims that the nominative Case (of the subject) is valued via φ-agreement with T, and the accusative Case (of the object) is valued via φ-agreement with V in Japanese. This line of studies also claims that the genitive Case is valued via φ-agreement with D (Ochi 2001, Hiraiwa 2005). To the best of my knowledge, they disregard how the dative Case is valued via φ-agreement.

I point out that this line of analysis faces a problem with multiple nominative / genitive constructions. Those who advocate the φ-agreement analysis of Case valuation in Japanese assume the [+multiple] feature concerning Agree (Ura 2000, Hiraiwa 2005). The [+multiple] feature enables a head to probe multiple goals. In multiple nominative constructions, such as (1a), [uφ] on T has multiple agreement with [vφ] on nominals. This is schematically illustrated in (1b). Consequently, [uCase] on the nominals receive the nominative Case value.

(1) a. Bummeikoku-ga   dansei-ga heikinjumyoo-ga
       developed.countries-NOM men-NOM average.longevity-NOM
       mijika-i.
       short-PRES
       Lit. 'Developed countries, men, average longevity is short.'

                                                          (Kuno 1973: 34)

   b. [NP$_{1[v\varphi, NOM]}$ NP$_{2[v\varphi, NOM]}$ NP$_{3[v\varphi, NOM]}$…[…V]-T$_{[u\varphi]}$…]…

                                                Multiple Agree(T, NP$_1$, NP$_2$, NP$_3$)
                                                (adapted from Hiraiwa 2005)

However, the postulation of such features is merely an *ad hoc* stipulation. I demonstrated that we need no such features to derive multiple subject constructions in Chapter 2.

I argue that Case valuation is not tied to φ-agreement in Japanese. In this book, I follow Zushi's (2014, 2016) analysis of Case valuation via merger.

Zushi's rules presume that Case is valued when a nominal phrase merges with a head. I modified Zushi's (2016) rules slightly in Chapter 3, as presented in (2a-c), to make them compatible with the proposals in Chapter 2.

(2)   The revised Case valuation rules:
   a.   When a nominal phrase becomes the sister of V, its Case feature is valued as accusative.
   b.   When a nominal phrase becomes the sister of *v* or *n*, its Case feature is valued as nominative or genitive.
   c.   Otherwise (i.e., when a nominal phrase becomes the sister of other heads), the Case feature of a nominal phrase is valued as dative.

I have already indicated that all canonical Case patterns in Japanese are derived via the rules in (2) in Chapter 3. I have demonstrated that Case valuation in Japanese does not require φ-agreement. In summary, I argued that Case in Japanese is not valued as a reflex of φ-agreement but is valued via sister relations created by merger and Transfer.

4.3.   Nominative / Genitive Conversion (NGC) (Hiraiwa 2001, 2005)

NGC is a phenomenon in which a nominative subject optionally alternates with a genitive subject in nominal complements and relative clauses in Japanese. The data are presented in (3). Hiraiwa (2001, 2005) proposes that genitive assignment in NGC is achieved by φ-agreement. He argues that *rentai-kei* 'adnominal form (ADN)' of the predicate is a key to specifying the structural Case on a DP as genitive (Hiraiwa 2001: 71).

(3)   Nominative / Genitive Conversion (NGC):
   a.   John-no / ga   suki-na   ongaku-wa blues da.
         John-GEN / NOM like-ADN music-TOP blues COP
         'The music that John likes is the Blues.'
   b.   John-no / ga   onkoo-na   koto-wa yuumei   da.
         John-GEN / NOM gentle-ADN fact-TOP well.known COP
         'It is well-known that John is gentle.'

   c. John-wa Mary-no / ga   yom-u-yori   takusan-no-hon-o
       John-TOP Mary-GEN / NOM read-ADN-than many-GEN-book-ACC
       yom-da.
       read-PAST
       'John read more books than Mary did.'

   d. John-wa ame-no / ga   yam-u-made ofisu-ni i-ta.
       John-TOP rain-GEN / NOM stop-ADN-till office-at be-PAST
       'John was at the office until the rain stopped.'

             (adapted from Hiraiwa 2001: 78, 83, cf. Watanabe 1996)

Specifically, he claims that the V-(*v*-)T-C amalgam realizes as the adnominal form, in which φ-features are copied from T onto C. Hiraiwa (2001, 2005) proposes that the φ-agreement between C and the subject DP specifies the structural Case as genitive. He assumes that nominative Case is assigned to nominals via φ-agreement with T. As the amalgamation is not obligatory, the NGC is optional in Hiraiwa's (2001, 2005) account.

    I argue that Hiraiwa's (2001, 2005) proposal does not support the claim that φ-agreement exists in Japanese. I propose an alternative analysis of NGC and argue that it is not φ-agreement that values nominative / genitive Case in NGC. Maki and Uchibori (2008: 203) indicate that examples of Hiraiwa (2001) that appear head-nounless such as (3c) and (3d) are instances of NGC where the head noun is implicit. Their data are presented in (4), where *-no* 'NM (NOMINAL(IZER))' in the boldface is either a noun itself (as it is inter-changeable with ***teido*** 'degree' in (4a)) or a nominalizer, which makes the en-tire clause nominal (Maki and Uchibori 2008: 203).[1]

---

[1] Hirata (2011) and Kobayashi (2012) provide data like (i), in which the predicate is not of the adnominal form but of the continuative form (*ren'yoo-kei*) *tsukamari-* 'catch'.

  (i) Hannin-ga / no   tsukamari-sidai   renraku-o kur-e.
      criminal-NOM / GEN capture-as.soon.as call-ACC give-IMP
      'Give me a call, as soon as the criminal is captured.'

                (Kobayashi 2012: 8)

This sort of data is problematic to Hiraiwa's (2001) generalization that the adnominal form licenses genitive Case of the subject in NGC. At the same time, the data in (i) poses a problem to our alternative analysis. Since *-no* or some other nominal element cannot be in-serted to the subordinate clause, as in (ii), there is no evidence that a nominal element li-censes NGC in (i).

(4) NGC data containing covert nominals:

    a. John-wa [Mary-ga / no   yonda(-*teido* / *no*) yori]
       John-TOP Mary-NOM / GEN read-degree / NM   than
       takusan-no hon-o   yom-da.
       many-GEN book-ACC read-PAST
       'John read more books than Mary did.'

    b. John-wa ame-ga / no   yamu(-*toki* / *zikan*)
       John-TOP rain-NOM / GEN stop-time / time
       made ofisu-ni i-ta.
       until office-at be-PAST
       'John was at the office until the rain stopped.'

    c. [Boku-ga / no omow(-*no*)-ni], John-wa
       I-NOM / GEN think-NM-DAT   John-TOP
       Mary-ga   sukini chigaina-i.
       Mary-NOM like   must-PRES
       'I think that John likes Mary.'

    d. Kono atari-wa [hi-ga / no   kureru(-*no*)
       this   around-TOP sun-NOM / GEN go.down-NM
       ni-ture]   hiekondeku-ru.
       DAT-go.together become.colder-PRES
       'It gets chillier around here as the sun goes down.'

    e. John-wa [toki-ga / no   tatsu(-*no*)-to tomo-ni]
       John-TOP time-NOM / GEN pass-NM-AND together-DAT
       Mary-no   koto-o   wasurete-ik-ta.
       Mary-GEN thing-ACC forget-go-PAST
       'Mary slipped out of John's memory as the time went by.'

(ii) *Hannin-no   tsukamari-*no* / *toki*-sidai   renraku-o kur-e.
     criminal-GEN capture-NM / time-as.soon.as call-ACC give-IMP

This type of example remains problematic to both Hiraiwa's (2001, 2005) approach and the present alternative analysis.

    f.   [John-ga / no   ku-ru(-**no**)-to ko-nai(-**no**)-to]   de-wa

        John-NOM / GEN come-NM-AND come-NEG-NM-AND at-TOP

        ootigai   da.

        greatly.different COP.PRES

        'It makes a great difference whether John comes or not.'

            (adapted from Maki and Uchibori 2008: 203, cf. Harada 2002)

Most of the sentences in (4) contain -**no** 'NM'. It seems that only -**no** and some other nominals can be implicit in certain environments.[2]

    I argue that the distribution of NGC can be accounted for with no recourse to φ-agreement. I assume with Maki and Uchibori (2008) that the data set of NGCs provided by Hiraiwa (2001, 2005), presented in (3), includes silent nominals, as exemplified in (4). Here, I concur with Zushi (2016) that Case is valued in the sister relations created by the merger in Japanese, as demonstrated in (5). The structure of the NGC constructions is shown in (6).

---

[2] Silent TIME is found in other constructions as well. Kayne (2003, 2016) claims that the silent TIME exists in (ia). This TIME can be overtly spelled out, as shown in (ib). The same applies to (ic) and (id).

  (i)   Sentences with silent TIME:
      a.   They'll be there in two hours (TIME).
      b.   They'll be there in two hours' time.
      c.   They'll leave (AT A) soon (TIME).
      d.   ?They'll leave at the soonest time possible.

                                   (Kayne 2016: 14)

Similarly, Takahashi (2015) claims that silent TOKI 'time' exists in some gapless relative clauses in Japanese. The set of data below (iia–c) implies that silent TOKI can be found in constructions other than those involving NGC in (4).

  (ii) Data with silent TOKI 'TIME' in Japanese:
      a.   Sakana-ga koge-ru (toki-no) nioi
          fish-NOM   burn-PRES time-GEN smell
          'The smell of fish getting burnt'
      b.   Hoochoo-de kit-ta (toki-no) kizuato
          knife-by   cut-PAST time-GEN scar
          'A scar from a knife cut'
      c.   Juusu-o   kat-ta   (toki-no) otsuri
          juice-ACC buy-PAST time-GEN change
          'Change for buying juice'

                                   (Takahashi 2015: 404)

(5)   The revised Case valuation rules: (=2)

    a.   When a nominal phrase becomes the sister of V, its Case feature is valued as accusative.

    b.   When a nominal phrase becomes the sister of v or n, its Case feature is valued as nominative or genitive.

    c.   Otherwise (i.e., when a nominal phrase becomes the sister of other heads), the Case feature of a nominal phrase is valued as dative.

(6)   [nP [[...nP...V v...] N] n]

Here, I extend Nagamori's (2020) suggestion. When the nP receives genitive Case, Nagamori (2020: 126) notes that it raises to [Spec, n] first, and then the multiple Transfer (see my proposal in Chapter 2) subsequently creates a configuration {nP, n}, as in (7a-c). According to the Case valuation rule in (5b), the Case of nP is valued as genitive. Nagamori (2020) claims that when the nP receives nominative Case, it remains in the verbal domain. As he notes, the optionality of NGC is captured by the free application of internal Merge (cf. Fukui and Nishigauchi 1992).

(7)   a.   [nP [[...nP...V v...] N] n]

    b.   [nP [[...nP...V v...] N] n] (transferred domain)

    c.   [nP n]

    cf.   [[[...nP...V v...] N] n]

The analysis precludes unwanted results such as *o-no* conversion and *ni-no* conversion. *O-no* conversion and *ni-no* conversion are not possible in Japanese, as illustrated in (8a-b) and (8c-d). The Case feature on a nominal phrase is immediately valued when the phrase becomes the sister of a head, according to the rules in (5). *O-no* conversion does not occur because an nP receives accusative Case in the base position. Once Case is valued, its value is fixed (contra Nagamori 2020). Therefore, even if the relevant nP is scrambled to the edge of n, it does not receive genitive Case from n.

(8)   The absence of *o-no* and *ni-no* conversions in Japanese:

    a.   Taro-ga   ringo-o   tabe-ta.

        Taro-NOM apple-ACC eat-PAST

        'Taro ate an apple.'

b. Ringo-o / *no   tabe-ta   Taro   (*o-no*)
    apple-ACC / GEN eat-PAST   Taro
    'Taro, who ate an apple'

c. Hanako-ga   daigaku-ni   shorui-o   okur-ta.
    Hanako-NOM   university-DAT   paper-ACC   send-PAST
    'Hanako sent a paper to the university.'

d. Daigaku-ni / *no   (Hanako-ga)   okur-ta   shorui   (*ni-no*)
    university-DAT / GEN Hanako-NOM   send-PAST paper
    'A paper that Hanako sent to the university'

The same applies to *ni-no* conversion. Since Transfer applies to $\{nP_1\text{-}o, V\}$
(the complement of Appl) in (9a), nP_2 derivationally becomes the sister of
Appl, as in (9b). As the Case value of nP_2 is fixed as dative, *ni-no* conversion does not occur.[3]

(9) a.

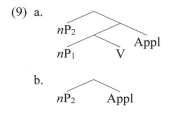

    b.

One may speculate whether the current analysis precludes *ga-no*
conversion. However, this is not the case. Transfer applies as soon as a
phase is completed (Richards 2007, Chomsky 2008, among others). I assume

---

[3] Takaomi Kato (p.c.) noted that if nP_2 merges internally with the edge of the structure in
(9a), then Appl may not be able to value the Case feature of nP_2 as they are not sisters. I
claim that such a super-short distance movement is prohibited in the derivation. Saito and
Murasugi (1999) and Grohmann (2011) posit the ban on such super-short distance movement, as in (i). I follow their assumption to preclude such movement described above.

(i) *[XP$_i$ [t_i Y...]]

                                                    (adapted from Grohmann 2011: 264)

This ban on super-short distance movement is independently proposed to explain the un-
grammaticality of such data as in (iic).

(ii) a. (I think that) John likes Mary.
     b. (I think that) Mary, John likes *t*.
     c. *(I think that) John, *t* likes Mary.

                                                    (Saito and Murasugi 1999: 182)

that v in Japanese, an agglutinative language, has a morphological requirement that enforces T or N to merge with the edge of vP for verbal conjugation/ tense-marking before Transfer applies. In other words, v is a phase head that requires T or N to be merged with vP in order for Transfer to apply.[4] Thus, after the completion of vP, N is introduced in (10a) before Transfer applies. Then, subject nP$_3$ internally merges with the edge, as in (10b). Thereafter, Transfer of the complement of v (i.e., {nP$_2$-ni, Appl}) occurs, as demonstrated in (10c). Following this, the next higher phase head n is introduced, as in (10d).[5] Subsequently, nP$_3$ moves to the edge of n, as presented in (10e). Transfer of the complement of n occurs. Finally, the structure will be like (10f), in which the subject nP$_3$ becomes the sister of n. According to the rule in (5b), nP$_3$ receives genitive Case.

(10) a.

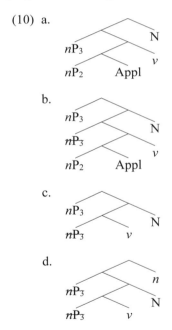

b.

c.

d.

---

[4] I would like to thank Hiroki Narita (p.c.) for pointing out this possibility.
[5] I assume that the lower copy of nPs does not receive Case. In other words, [uCase] on the lower copy is invisible from the Case valuation rules in (2).

e.

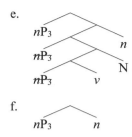

f.

         nP$_3$ n

In sum, Hiraiwa's (2001) proposal on NGC does not support the claim that Japanese has φ-agreement, as there is an alternative analysis of NGC in Japanese with no recourse to φ-agreement.[6]

---

[6] With the so-called Transitivity Restriction (Watanabe 1996) observed in (i), Hiraiwa (2005) presents a generalization in (ii).

  (i) a.   Kinoo   John-ga   hon-o   kaw-ta.
             yesterday John-NOM book-ACC buy-PAST
             'John bought a book yesterday.'
      b. *Kinoo   John-no   hon-o   kaw-ta   mise
             yesterday John-GEN book-ACC buy-PAST store
             'The store where John bought a book yesterday'
    cf. Kinoo   John-ga   hon-o   kaw-ta   mise
             yesterday John-NOM book-ACC buy-PAST store

  (ii) ACC-NOM generalization:
      Realization of morphological accusative case is contingent on structural nominative Case.

                                      (adapted from Hiraiwa 2005: 145)

Harada (2002: 145), on the other hand, states that there is no such thing as Transitivity Restriction; however, Harada (1971) posits a broader condition, presented in (iii) and based on observations in (iv), in which the sentences are degraded due to the presence of non-accusative phrases. The intervener refers to an element that intervenes between the subject and the predicate (*hon-o* 'book-ACC' in (ib)) in the NGC constructions.

  (iii) The nounier the intervener, the less acceptable is the output of Ga-No Conversion.
                                    (Harada 1976: 36 (30))

  (iv) a. ??Dare-mo [[Taro-no   awatete   kaer-ta]-koto]-ni
           who-also   Taro-GEN hurriedly return-PAST-fact-DAT
           ki-ga   tsuka-nakat-ta.
           attention-NOM   pay-NEG-PAST
           'Nobody noticed that Taro hurriedly went back.'
      b.*?Sachiko-wa [[otto-no   Amerika-e ki-ta]-koto]-o
           Sachiko-TOP husband-GEN America-to come-PAST-fact-ACC

4.4.   Person Restriction (Miyagawa 2010, Obata and Sugimura 2014, 2019)

Miyagawa (2010) and Obata and Sugimura (2014, 2019) argue that there is φ-agreement in Japanese based on the observations of data such as (11a–b) (cf. Nitta 1991).

(11) a. *Boku / Kimi / *Taro-wa sonna-koto kinisu-ru-***na***.   (Prohibition)
        I / You / Taro-TOP   such-fact   mind-PRES-PROH
        'I / You / Taro must not mind such a thing.'

     b. Boku / *Kimi / *Kare-ga sugu ik-***oo***.   (Intention)
        I / You / He-NOM   now go-INT
        'I / You / He will go now.'

(Ueda 2008: 134)

In (11a), the modal head -*na* 'PROHIBITION' is not compatible with the first- or third-person subject. In (11b), the modal head -*(y)oo* 'INTENTION' is only compatible with the first-person subject. They consider these observations evidence to claim that Japanese has φ-agreement.

Obata and Sugimura (2019) propose that the Person features of the modal heads are specified as [2nd] in (12a) and as [1st] in (12b), while the Number features are unvalued. The [uNumber] on the C / Modal probes down into the structure and φ-agreement occurs with the subject, whose Person feature matches that of the C / Modal. In order for the Number agreement to occur, Obata and Sugimura (2019) assume that the Person features of the subject and modal head must be identical.

(12) a. [...[DP_{[Num][2nd]} T [...]] Mod / C_{[uNum][2nd]}]   (Prohibition: -*na*)
     b. [...[DP_{[Num][1st]} T [...]] Mod / C_{[uNum][1st]}]   (Intention: -*(y)oo*)

Obata and Sugimura (2014, 2019) further claim that the Person restriction is

---

sir-tei-ta.
know-ASP-PAST
'Sachiko was aware that her husband came to America.'
(adapted from Harada 2002: 130 (13–14))

Since the apparent restriction seems unrelated to φ-agreement, and it has been known that there are idiolectal variations since Harada (1976), I do not discuss this in this book.

also triggered by the *give*-type verbs (*age-* and *kure-* 'give'). The data are presented in (13a) and (13b). In (13a), *kure-* imposes a restriction on the subject as either [2nd person] or [3rd person], while in (13b), *age-* only allows the indirect object with [2nd person] or [3rd person].

(13) a. *Watashi / Anata / Hanako-ga Taro-ni   hon-o   kure-ta.
        I / You / Hanako-NOM   Taro-DAT book-ACC give-PAST
        'I / You / Hanako gave Taro the book.'

    b. Hanako-ga   *watashi / anata / Taro-ni hon-o   age-ta.
        Hanako-NOM I / You / Taro-DAT   book-ACC give-PAST
        'Hanako gave me / you / Taro the book.'

(Obata and Sugimura 2014: 114)

Obata and Sugimura (2014, 2019) propose that the *give*-type verbs are unspecified for Person features as [2nd] or [3rd], and their Number features have no value. They undergo verb-movement to T, and then the unvalued features on V probe for the agree-mates. Finally, φ-agreement occurs between the verbal amalgam with *-kure* 'give' and the subject in (14a) as well as the verbal amalgam with *-age* 'give' and the object in (14b).

(14) a. [SUBJ$_{[Num][2nd / 3rd]}$...OBJ... [V$_{[uNum][2nd\ or\ 3rd]}$-v-T]]   (=13a)
       ⬆_____| agreement

    b. [SUBJ...OBJ$_{[Num][2nd / 3rd]}$... [V$_{[uNum][2nd\ or\ 3rd]}$-v-T]]   (=13b)
       ⬆_____| agreement

    I argue that the abovementioned observations of Obata and Sugimura (2014, 2019) do not support the claim that Japanese has φ-agreement. First, I argue against the analysis of modal agreement. The prohibition in (11a) is a type of imperatives. Imperatives are used for the addressee; hence, it semantically or pragmatically cannot have a first- or third-person subject. An intentional modal in (11b), on the other hand, requires the first-person subject since it shows the addresser's intention; hence, it semantically or pragmatically requires the speaker, the first person, as its subject. That said, the unacceptability of (11a) and (11b) may not be due to ungrammaticality (i.e., existence of [uF]), but may be caused by semantic ill-formedness at the C-I interface.[7] Therefore, Obata and Sugimura's (2014, 2019) evidence for the claim that

---

[7] I thank Takaomi Kato (p.c.) for bringing this possibility to my attention.

Japanese has φ-agreement is inconclusive.

Moreover, Obata and Sugimura's (2014, 2019) account has conceptual and empirical problems. I emphasize that it is just a stipulation to assume that the probe X and the goal Y Agree regarding a certain feature only if the values of the other features of X and Y match. Let us call this the feature-matching condition on Agree. Obata and Sugimura limit the scope of this condition to a set of φ-features (e.g., [uNumber] and [vNumber] Agree only if the values of [vPerson] match between X and Y), but there is no principled reason to restrict the scope of their feature-matching condition to a set of φ-features. Once they posit such a condition on Agree, features such as Case and other semantic features such as [+animate] would also need to match between the probe and the goal. This leads to a significant undergeneration problem. A canonical sentence, such as *John ate an apple* cannot be derived, as features such as Case and [+animate] do not match between *John* and T (only *John* has both [uCase] and [+animate]).

Next, I argue against the analysis of *give*-type verbs. I maintain that Kuno and Kaburaki's (1977) theory of Empathy summarized in (15) can also explain the contrasts in (13).[8] The sentences in (16a) and (16b) are different in meaning: the speaker's point of view (Empathy in (15a)) differs according to the verb form. In (16a), the speaker's point of view is focused on the agent *Hanako*, while in (15b), it is focused on the recipient *Taro*. When *age-* is used in (13b), the speaker's empathy is focused on the subject; hence, the first person cannot appear in the object position, violating the requirement of Speech-Act Empathy Hierarchy in (15b), which states that the empathy focus is always on the speaker themselves if the speaker is in the sentence. When it turns to *kure-* in (13a), the speaker's empathy is focused on the object. Therefore, the use of the first-person subject obtains an unacceptable result in violation of the requirement in (15b).

(15) a. **Empathy**:

Empathy is the speaker's identification, with varying degrees (ranging from 0 to 1), with a person who participates in the event that they describe in a sentence.

---

[8] I would like to thank Takaomi Kato (p.c.) for referring me to Kuno and Kaburaki (1977).

b. **Speech-Act Empathy Hierarchy**:
It is not possible for the speaker to empathize more with someone else than with him / herself.
(adapted from Kuno and Kaburaki 1977: 628, 631)

(16) a.   Hanako-ga   Taro-ni   hon-o   age-ta.
Hanako-NOM Taro-DAT book-ACC give-PAST
'Hanako gave a book to Taro.'

b.   Hanako-ga   Taro-ni   hon-o   kure-ta.
Hanako-NOM Taro-DAT book-ACC give-PAST
'Hanako gave a book to Taro.'

Other independent evidence also reveals that Empathy is necessary in linguistic theory. I focus on the nature of *zibun* 'self' and its interaction with
deictic verbs *ku-* 'come' and *ik-* 'go' (Kuno and Kaburaki 1977: 637). The
data are presented in (17).

(17) a.   John$_i$-wa [zyuu-nen-mae-ni Mary-ga
John-TOP ten-years-ago-at Mary-NOM
zibun$_i$-o tazune-te *ki*-ta   ie]-de
self-ACC visit-ASP come-PAST house-at
ima-wa   koohukuni kurasi-tei-mas-u.
now-TOP happily   live-ASP-POL-PRES
'John now lives happily in the house where Mary came to visit
him ten years ago.'

b. *John$_i$-wa [zyuu-nen-mae-ni Mary-ga
John-TOP ten-years-ago-at Mary-NOM
zibun$_i$-o tazune-te *it*-ta   ie]-de
self-ACC visit-ASP go-PAST house-at
ima-wa   koohukuni kurasi-tei-mas-u.
now-TOP happily   live-ASP-POL-PRES
'John now lives happily in the house where Mary went to visit
him ten years ago.'

(Kuroda 1973)

Kuno and Kaburaki (1977: 637) claim that the empathy relation must be con-
sistent in a sentence. In (17a) and (17b), *zibun* refers to John. *Ku-* 'come' is
a deictic verb that requires the object to be the focus of the speaker's empathy,
and *ik-* 'go' is another deictic verb that makes the subject the focus of the

speaker's empathy. In (17a), *ku-* 'come' is used in the relative clause, which makes the object *zibun* (=*John*) the speaker's focus of empathy. In other words, the speaker empathizes with *John* in the relative clause. In the main clause, as *John* is the subject, the speaker's focus of empathy is on *John*. Therefore, the speaker's empathy foci are on *John* both in the relative and main clauses, which ensures the consistency of empathy foci in the embedded and main clauses. In (17b), *ik-* 'go' is used in the relative clause, which makes the subject *Mary* the speaker's focus of empathy. In other words, the speaker empathizes with *Mary* in the relative clause. In the main clause, since *John* is the subject, the speaker's empathy is focused on *John*. Therefore, (17b) involves an irreconcilable conflict about the focus of empathy, in which the focus of empathy is on *John* in the main clause, while it is on *Mary* in the relative clause. To explain the contrast between minimal pairs like (17a–b), Kuno and Kaburaki (1977) emphasize that the concept of Empathy is necessary. This indicates that Empathy is independently required in linguistic theory.

To summarize, Obata and Sugimura's (2014, 2019) observations and analysis do not support their claim that φ-agreement exists in Japanese, as the Person restriction can be explained with no recourse to syntactic agreement. Moreover, there is an alternative analysis of Person restrictions with *give*-type verbs based on Empathy (Kuno and Kaburaki 1977).

4.5.   Honorification as φ-agreement (Toribio 1990, Ura 2000)

Ura (2000), citing Toribio (1990), claims that honorific affixation is an instance of φ-agreement in Japanese. The relevant data are presented in (18a) and (18b). To be more precise, they assume that subject-honorification is induced by the Spec-Head agreement of φ-features (Ura 2000: 100).

> (18) a.   Yamada-sensei-ga   o-warai-ni   nar-ta.
>   Yamada-prof.-NOM HON-laugh-to become-PAST
>   'Prof. Yamada laughed.'
>   b.   Yamada-sensei-ga   gakusei-o   o-tasuke-ni   nar-ta.
>   Yamada-prof.-NOM student-ACC HON-help-to become-PAST
>   'Prof. Yamada helped the student.'
>
> (adapted from Shibatani 1978b: 55, Ura 2000: 100)

Although honorific agreement in Toribio's (1990) and Ura's (2000) analyses is achieved via Spec-Head feature checking in the GB era, it can be reinterpreted as the agreement between [uφ] and [vφ] that the current study is investigating. Suppose that [uφ] resides in T, and the corresponding [vφ] is on the subject *n*P. The [uφ] on T probes into the complement *v*P, and then finds the corresponding [vφ] on the subject. Thereafter, Agree occurs between the [uφ] and the [vφ], which morphologically realizes as an honorific affix on the predicate, as in (18).

I argue that honorification is irrelevant to φ-agreement in Japanese. First, it is evident that honorification phenomena are distinct from φ-agreement in English and other Indo-European languages (cf. Niinuma 2003: 60). The φ-agreement involves features such as [Person] and [Number] (and sometimes [Gender]) in these languages. However, the honorific morphology is completely different from that of φ-agreement. Honorific morphemes indicate the social status of the referents. Fukui (1995) points out that it is highly questionable whether such morphology should be treated as instances of φ-morphology, which indicates Person and Number (and sometimes Gender) information of the referents.

Second, the honorific morphology need not appear in the conversational situation where the subject has a high social status.[9] The sentences in (18) are never ungrammatical without the honorific morphology, as in (19a–b). If φ-agreement occurs in honorific constructions, then it is expected that the data in (19a–b) would be totally ungrammatical like the data in (20a–b). Because the nature of honorific morphology is completely different from that of φ-agreement morphology, the data in (18) do not serve as evidence for φ-agreement in Japanese.

(19) a. Yamada-sensei-ga waraw-ta.
          Yamada-prof.-NOM laugh-PAST
          'Prof. Yamada laughed.'
      b. Yamada-sensei-ga gakusei-o   tasuke-ta.
          Yamada-prof.-NOM student-ACC help-PAST
          'Prof. Yamada helped a student.'

---

[9] I would like to thank Takaomi Kato (p.c.) for pointing this out to me, crediting the observations and insights to Naoki Fukui.

(20) a. *John laugh. (cf. John laughs / laughed.)

     b. *Mary help her students. (cf. Mary helps / helped her students.)

One may say that agreement is optional in honorification. In other words, [uφ] can be on the predicate only in some cases. It is impossible to empirically distinguish this possibility from the claim that honorification has nothing to do with φ-features or φ-feature agreement. Since these two different possibilities are empirically tied, I conclude that the claim that honorific morphology is irrelevant to φ-agreement is correct here for the conceptual reasons stated previously.

Before commencing with the next section, a note on Boeckx and Niinuma (2004) is required. They claim that object-honorification, as depicted in (21a) and (21b), in Japanese is an instance of φ-agreement. Since the same counterarguments as above apply, I do not discuss their observations or analysis in detail here. Furthermore, Bobaljik and Yatsushiro (2006) present extensive arguments against Boeckx and Niinuma (2004) (cf. Boeckx 2006).

(21) a. Taro-ga   Tanaka-sensei-o   o-tasuke-si-ta.

         Taro-NOM Tanaka-prof.-ACC HON-help-do-PAST

         'Taro helped Prof. Tanaka.'

     b. Hanako-ga   Tanaka-sensei-ni Mary-o   go-syookaisi-ta.

         Hanako-NOM Tanaka-prof.-DAT Mary-ACC HON-introduce-PAST

         'Hanako introduced Mary to Prof. Tanaka.'

(Boeckx and Niinuma 2004: 456)

4.6.   Allocutive Agreement (Miyagawa 2017)

Miyagawa (2017) argues that Japanese shows allocutive agreement like Basque and other languages. Assuming that C-to-T feature-inheritance occurs in English, but significantly not in Japanese, Miyagawa proposes that C with φ-features raises to the domain of SpeechActP (**SAP**), more precisely to the small sa-head and consequently to the SA-head. The φ-features then serve as an allocutive probe. The φ-features of the SA-head probe for the HEARER, a null nominal (interlocutor) with a second-person feature, in [Spec, saP]. Then they undergo φ-agreement, which realizes as a polite form -*des* / *mas*

'POL' in Japanese.[10]   The derivation is illustrated in (22a–c) and the data are in (23).   Miyagawa (2017) states that when the hearer is present (in conversational situation / Speech Act), *-des / mas* must be present, as in (23b).

(22) a.   [$_{CP}$ ...TP C$_{[\varphi]}$]
  b.   [$_{SAP}$ SPEAKER [$_{saP}$ HEARER [$_{CP}$ ...TP C$_{[\varphi]}$] sa] SA]
  c.   [$_{SAP}$ SPEAKER [$_{saP}$ HEARER [$_{CP}$ ...TP ~~C$_{[\varphi]}$~~] ~~C$_{[\varphi]}$~~-sa] C$_{[\varphi]}$-sa-SA]

                (Miyagawa 2017: 26–29)

(23) a.   Watashi-wa piza-o tabe-ru.
    I-TOP   pizza-ACC eat-PRES
    'I eat pizza.'
  b.   Watashi-wa piza-o tabe-***mas***-u.
    I-TOP   pizza-ACC eat-POL-PRES
    'I eat pizza.'

                (Miyagawa 2017: 19)

I argue that Miyagawa's (2017) proposal does not provide evidence for φ-agreement in Japanese.   The polite form need not appear in the conversational situation where the hearer is someone who the speaker should show respect to.   It is true that the lack of *-des / mas* may make the sentence (i.e., (23a)) sound a little rude, but never ungrammatical.   If φ-agreement needs to occur in (23a) but does not, then it is expected that the data become ungrammatical like the English example in (24a).   Given that (23a) is grammatical, the data in (23b) should not be construed as evidence for φ-agreement in Japanese.

(24) a.   *John like cats.
  b.   John likes cats.

4.7.   Summary

In this chapter, I reviewed five different arguments for φ-agreement in

---

[10] Likewise, SPEAKER in Miyagawa (2017) refers to a silent nominal that has a first-person feature.

Japanese: (i) Case valuation, (ii) nominative / genitive conversion, (iii) Person restriction, (iv) honorification, and (v) apparent allocutive agreement. I offered rebuttals to each. By demonstrating that none of them is persuasive enough, Chapter 4 supports the argument that Japanese lacks [uφ] in the lexicon.

　　Unvalued φ-features are, by definition, uninterpretable at the interfaces, and are, therefore, irrelevant to LF and the human thought system (Fukui 1990). As such, they have no conceptual necessity (Chomsky 2007b: 5). The particular approach reviewed in this chapter assumes that languages in general, even those without overt evidence, have unvalued φ-features and agreement. Considering that there is no persuasive evidence for φ-features in Japanese, I conclude that it is not desirable to postulate them in Japanese.

Chapter 5

Conclusion

5.1. Summary of the Book

In this book, I argued for the following statement, which is part of the FPH: the presence / absence of agreement features of functional categories in the lexicon yields certain parametric variation. Throughout this book, I have shown that Japanese lacks [uφ] in the lexicon, supported by a few case studies and discussions in Chapters 2, 3, and 4 from a comparative perspective. In Chapter 1, I reviewed how the FPH (Fukui 1988, 1990, 1995, among others) emerged in the theory of language. Thereafter, I examined the literature on different approaches to the study of human language: Language Acquisition and Language Disorder. I argued that it is reasonable that functional categories are subject to variation in contrast to lexical categories. Furthermore, I demonstrated that it is not unnatural that agreement features of functional categories are also subject to variation. This argument is incompatible with the EH (Chomsky 2010, Berwick and Chomsky 2011, 2016, Boeckx 2016, among others), which states that cross-linguistic variation stems only at the PF-branch. Chapter 2 proposed an analysis of how several apparently unlabelable constructions in Japanese are labeled under the assumption that Japanese lacks [uφ] in the lexicon. I revealed that canonical sentences, multiple subject constructions, and (multiple) scrambling constructions in Japanese can all be derived without labeling failure by solving the {XP, YP} problem of Chomsky (2013). In Chapter 3, I proposed an exploratory generalization that languages with object-verb φ-agreement cannot have productive lexical VV-compounds. Thereafter, I provided a morphosyntactic analysis of why productive lexical VV-compounds are absent in English and other languages with object-verb φ-agreement. Importantly, I discussed how Case is licensed in Japanese, which lacks φ-agreement. Chapter 4 consists of extensive discussions on previous studies that argue for the presence of φ-agreement in Japanese. I carefully reviewed five different arguments for φ-agreement in Japanese, and then offered rebuttals to each of them. Showing that there is little substantive evidence for φ-agreement in Japanese, Chapter 4 further supports the argument that Japanese lacks [uφ] in its lexicon. Overall, I argued that Japanese lacks [uφ] in the lexicon, and the presence/absence of agreement features in the lexicon yields certain parametric variation. This book as a whole provides a counterargument to the EH.

5.2.   On Discourse Orientation and φ-agreement

Before concluding the book, I make some comments on the relation between the presence/absence of φ-features and discourse orientation in languages. The core argument in this book that Japanese lacks [uφ] implies that Fukui's (1988, 1995) insight and idea on a correlation between the absence of φ-features and discourse orientation are both conceptually and empirically preferable to Miyagawa's (2017) recent claim. A characterization of discourse-oriented languages is as follows in (1):

(1)   Discourse-oriented languages:
        Languages with a cluster of distinctive properties: topic-prominence, discourse-bound anaphors, and null-topics.

(adapted from Huang 1984)

I demonstrated that Japanese lacks φ-features. Likewise, Korean and Mandarin Chinese lack overt evidence of φ-agreement. Japanese, along with Korean and Mandarin Chinese, is a discourse-oriented language (Li and Thompson 1976, Tsao 1977, Huang 1984). On the other hand, Indo-European languages, including English, French, Italian and German, have φ-features and are non-discourse-oriented languages (i.e., sentence-oriented languages) (Li and Thompson 1976, among others).[1] Therefore, it can be concluded that there is a correlation between the presence / absence of φ-features and discourse orientation across languages.

The null topic construction is a typical trait of discourse-oriented languages; therefore, I take its presence as evidence for discourse orientation. Following Tsao's (1977) distinction between discourse- and sentence-prominent languages, Huang (1984) proposes the Null-topic Parameter, as presented in (2). Typical data of linguistic antecedent-less null arguments are provided in (3). Note that the relevant gap cannot be elliptic because it lacks an overt linguistic antecedent (Hankamer and Sag 1976).

(2)   Null-topic Parameter:
      Discourse-oriented languages have null-topics that license null arguments without linguistic antecedents. Non-discourse-oriented languages cannot license null arguments without linguistic antecedents.

(3)   Context: students heard footsteps from outside, just before the class.
      a.   Japanese:
           [e] kita.
           '[e] came.' (=The teacher came.)
      b.   English:
           *[e] came.

(adapted from Abe 2009)

Miyagawa (2017) attempts to derive the distinction between discourse-oriented and non-discourse-oriented languages under the assumption that all languages have φ-features and a δ-feature (a Topic / Focus feature) in their lexicon. He assumes that φ-features and a δ-feature are on C and can be inherited by T in the derivation. Furthermore, Miyagawa (2017) claims that Japanese has φ-features on C and that they Agree with the HEARER in the

---

[1] Huang (1984) suggests that German can also have a null topic. However, its nature and the parallelism between the data of Mandarin Chinese and German have been questioned by Paul (2017), among others. What Huang calls a "null topic" in German is contextually highly restricted, unlike in Japanese. Furthermore, it is different from that of Japanese, Korean, and Mandarin Chinese, as the former always requires a linguistic antecedent. Therefore, I conclude that the null topic in German is not a real one.

speech act phrases above CP, which were reviewed in Chapter 4. Moreover, he assumes that Japanese has a δ-feature bearing Topic/Focus functions on T. Miyagawa further claims that in English, φ-features are on T and a δ-feature is on C. In addition, he allows other combinations of features and functional heads, such as Dinka, which has both features on C. Note that Miyagawa (2017: 5) admits that Spanish has a δ-feature both on C and on T.

Miyagawa argues that a language is discourse-oriented if T inherits the whole δ-feature (Miyagawa 2017: 4). Spanish, Dinka, and English are not discourse-oriented languages unlike Japanese. Miyagawa's (2017) proposal presupposes that discourse orientation properties have no substantive correlation with the presence of φ-features. It is all a matter of free choice and combinations of two types of features and two functional heads: C and T. Therefore, his analysis does not capture the correlation between the absence of φ-features and discourse orientation in languages.

On the other hand, Fukui (1988, 1995) claims that the absence of φ-features and discourse orientation properties correlate with each other. Let us consider the null-topic construction, which is a typical trait of discourse-oriented languages, as a case study. Fukui (1988, 1995) proposes that in Japanese, which lacks substantive content of AGR, T, and C, clauses are projection of V. The projection of V seeks an element that is predicated of by it. Fukui argues that this element is an empty topic (Fukui 1995: 342). He concludes that "[a]n 'empty topic' is thus required as a consequence of the basic property of clauses as predicates in topic-prominent languages" (Fukui 1988: 269).

There are two reasons why Fukui's (1988, 1995) idea is preferable to Miyagawa's (2017). First, as we have seen in this book, Japanese lacks [uφ]; hence, Miyagawa's (2017) assumption that Japanese has φ-features on C does not hold. Second, Miyagawa's (2017) analysis misses an important correlation between the presence/absence of φ-features and discourse orientation in languages. Therefore, I conclude that Fukui's (1988, 1995) idea is both empirically and conceptually preferable to Miyagawa's (2017) analysis of discourse orientation.

One might consider whether Fukui's (1988, 1995) idea is incompatible with the proposals in this book, as Japanese has T (and C), and the clauses in Japanese are not the projection of V in the current analysis. I suggest that Fukui's (1988, 1995) insight can be restated under the assumptions of this book. Let us review Zushi's (2003) reinterpretation of Fukui's (1988, 1995) analysis that Japanese clauses are verbal. Following Fukui, she assumes that φ-features have nominal properties, and so the projection of T is argumental in English because it has φ-features. On the other hand, Japanese lacks φ-features on T; hence, the projection of the clauses is not argumental but predicative. She states that a null topic is licensed through predication with the predicative clause in Japanese (Zushi 2003: 593).

I restate Zushi's (2003) analysis as follows: CP in Japanese is predicative (non-argumental) for the lack of φ-features on C-T, which are nominal in nature. In English, CP is argumental in nature, since C-T has φ-features with nominal properties. In this analysis, if a clause lacks an overt argument, then the covert argument is identified with a null-topic in Japanese as in (4).

(4)   The null-topic operator is base-generated in the C-domain:
      [$_{CP}$ Op [$_{TP}$ [$_{vP}$ e [$_{VP}$ ... V] v] T] C]

The null-topic operator is licensed even when there is no covert argument in Japanese. The data are shown in (5), and the structure is depicted in (6). In (5), there is no overt topic *Hiroshima* in the sentences; however the interpretations are such that 'As for Hiroshima, the oyster is delicious' in (5a) and 'As for Hiroshima, is everyone rooting for Carp?' in (5b).

(5)   Context: watching a TV program featuring Hiroshima prefecture:
      a.   Kaki-ga   oishi-i   yo-ne.
           oyster-NOM delicious-PRES PRT-PRT
           'As for Hiroshima, the oyster is delicious, isn't it?'
      b.   Minna-ga   Kaapu-o ouensi-tei-ru   no?
           everyone-NOM Carp-ACC cheer-ASP-PRES Q
           'As for Hiroshima, is everyone rooting for Carp?'

(6)   The null-topic operator construction with overt arguments:
      [$_{CP}$ Op [$_{TP}$ [$_{vP}$ SUBJ [$_{VP}$ OBJ V] v] T] C]

Following Abe (2009), I assume that the null-topic operator is nominal with valued φ-features and receives its semantic content from the referent in discourse at the C-I interface after narrow syntax. After a merger of the null-topic operator in the C-domain in (4) and (6), the operator (nominal) and the clause (predicative due to the lack of φ-features in Japanese) creates a predication relation, as illustrated in (7). This is not possible in English and other φ-agreement languages because the clause is argumental due to the presence of φ-features.

(7)   Predication of the null-topic operator and the clause in Japanese:
[Op [[[SUBJ [OBJ V] v] T] C]]
|_____| predication

The current analysis based on Zushi (2003) captures Fukui's (1988, 1995) original idea and insight that Japanese clauses are predicative due to the lack of φ-features. Although the jury is still out on that, I leave further investigation of this line of analysis for future research.[2] In summary, the proposal in this book that Japanese lacks [uφ] indicates that Fukui's (1988, 1995) idea that the absence of φ-features has a correlation with discourse orientation across languages is conceptually and empirically preferable to Miyagawa's (2017) recent claim on discourse-orientation in languages.[3]

---

[2] We can observe that the overt topic in English fails to form a predication relation with clauses, as in (i).

(i)   *That book, John read it.   (cf. Speaking of / As for that book, John read it.)

However, considering sentences such as (ii), unsaturated phrases such as *Mary read* in English can be predicative in topicalization. I assume with Chomsky (1977, 1981), among many others, that topicalization in English is derived via the null operator movement, as illustrated in (iii). One may wonder why English does not allow the null topic with unsaturated predicative phrases such as *Mary read* in (iii).

(ii)   That book, Mary read.

(iii)   That book, [Op [Mary read t]].
               ▲_____|

Zushi (2003: 594) claims, following Rizzi (1997), that the null operator in (iii) is anaphoric in the sense that it links an antecedent and the bindee (through identification) in syntax. The topic (the antecedent) must have some referential value to identify the bindee. She states that if the topic (the antecedent) were null, no referential value could be given to the trace position bound by the operator in (iii). Therefore, the topic phrase cannot be null in clauses such as (iii) in English based on Zushi's (2003) analysis.

    Another possibly problematic case can be seen from the prediction that the null topic should be available when clauses in English lack φ-features. Such examples are infinitival clauses and small clauses (Toru Ishii p.c.). I leave this issue for future research.

[3] Since I claim that there is a correlation between the absence of φ-features and discourse-orientation, we need to test whether other languages without φ-agreement have properties of discourse orientation. However, this is a topic for future research.

5.3.   Final Remarks

Naoki Fukui (p.c.) notes that Language Change regarding φ-features occurs in one way: they disappear and do not emerge from scratch or become more complex during Language Change. In the same vein, Roberts (2018) and Roberts and Roussou (2003: 17) claim that Language Change occurs unidirectionally from the complex to the simple. More precisely, the agreement features disappear, but do not emerge in functional categories.

Agreement features are LF-uninterpretable and are, therefore, irrelevant to LF or the human thought system (Fukui 1990). Since they are not crucial for the design of human language as an instrument of thought (Fukui and Sakai 2003), it is natural to conclude that they are ultimately unnecessary for human language. Being unnecessary, it is reasonable to claim that [uφ] and other unvalued features are subject to disappearance in some languages, which yields certain language variations. This is exactly what I have argued for in this book.

If this argument is correct, it raises the question of why such unnecessary features were introduced to human language. This book presumes that functional categories and agreement features emerged later than lexical categories during Language Evolution (Progovac 2015). The reason they were introduced into human language is not obvious. It might be an instance of contingency, which often occurs in evolution in general. They may exist in some human languages for the sake of labeling the otherwise unlabelable symmetric structures, as Chomsky (2013, 2015b, c) assumes. I currently do not have an exact answer. Therefore, I leave this issue open for future research. This book leaves a number of issues open for future research. However, I hope that the arguments and discussions presented in this book contribute to gaining a better understanding of Japanese syntax, and ultimately, human language.

References

Abe, Jun. 2009. Identification of null arguments in Japanese. In Hiroto Hoshi (ed.), *The Dynamics of the Language Faculty: Perspectives from Linguistics and Cognitive Neuroscience*, 135–162. Tokyo: Kuroshio Publishers.

Anderson, Stephen. 1992. *A-morphous Morphology*. Cambridge: Cambridge University Press.

Baker, Mark. 1988. *Incorporation: A Theory of Grammatical Function Changing*. Chicago: University of Chicago Press.

Baker, Mark. 2003. *Lexical Categories: Verbs, Nouns and Adjectives*. Cambridge: Cambridge University Press.

Berwick, Robert, and Noam Chomsky. 2011. The biolinguistic program: the current state of its development. In Anna Maria Di Sciullo and Cedrick Boeckx (eds.), *The Biolinguistic Enterprise*, 19–41. Oxford: Oxford University Press

Berwick, Robert, and Noam Chomsky. 2016. *Why Only Us: Language and Evolution*. Cambridge, MA: MIT Press.

Bhattacharya, Tanmoy. 1999. Specificity in the Bangla DP. In Rajendra Singh (ed.). *Yearbook on South Asian Languages and Linguistics, vol 2*, 71–99. New Delhi/London: SAGE Publications.

Bobaljik, Jonathan, and Kazuko Yatsushiro. 2006. Problems with honorification-as-agreement in Japanese: A reply to Boeckx and Niinuma. *Natural Language & Linguistic Theory* 24(2), 355–384.

Boeckx, Cedric. 2006. Honorification as agreement. *Natural Language & Linguistic Theory* 24(2), 385–398.

Boeckx, Cedric. 2011. Approaching parameters from below. In Anna Maria Di Sciullo and Cedric Boeckx (eds.), *The Biolinguistic Enterprise: New Perspectives on the Evolution and Nature of the Human Language Faculty*, 205–221. Oxford: Oxford

University Press.

Boeckx, Cedric. 2014. *Elementary Syntactic Structures: Prospects of a Feature-free Syntax*. Cambridge: Cambridge University Press.

Boeckx, Cedric. 2016. Considerations pertaining to the nature of logodiversity. In Luis Eguren, Olga Fernandez-Soriano and Amaya Mendikoetxea (eds.), *Rethinking Parameters*, 64–104. Oxford: Oxford University Press.

Boeckx, Cedric, and Fumikazu Niinuma. 2004. Conditions on agreement in Japanese. *Natural Language & Linguistic Theory* 22(3), 453–480.

Borer, Hagit. 1984. *Parametric Syntax: Case Studies in Semitic and Romance Languages*. Dordrecht: Foris Publications.

Borsley, Robert, Tallerman, Maggie, and David Willis. 2007. *The Syntax of Welsh*. Cambridge: Cambridge University Press.

Chomsky, Noam. 1977. On Wh-movement. In Peter Culicover, Thomas Wasow and Adrian Akmajian (eds.), *Formal Syntax*, 71–132. New York: Academic Press.

Chomsky, Noam. 1980. Discussion. In Massimo Piattelli-Palmarini. (ed.), *Language and Learning. The Debate between Jean Piaget and Noam Chomsky*, 73–83. London: Routledge and Kegan Paul.

Chomsky, Noam. 1981. *Lectures on Government and Binding*. Dordrecht: Foris.

Chomsky, Noam. 1995. *The Minimalist Program*. Cambridge, MA: MIT Press.

Chomsky, Noam. 2000. Minimalist inquiries: The framework. In Roger Martin, David Michaels and Juan Uriagereka (eds.), *Step by Step: Essays on Minimalist Syntax in Honor of Howard Lasnik*, 89–155. Cambridge, MA: MIT Press.

Chomsky, Noam. 2001. Derivation by phase. In Michael Kenstowicz (ed.), *Ken Hale: A Life in Language*, 1–52. Cambridge, MA: MIT Press

Chomsky, Noam. 2004. Beyond explanatory adequacy. In Adriana Beletti (ed.), *The Cartography of Syntactic Structures, Vol. 3, Structures and Beyond*, 104–131. Oxford: Oxford University Press.

Chomsky, Noam. 2007a. Biolinguistic explorations: Design, development, evolution. *International Journal of Philosophical Studies*, 15(1), 1–21.

Chomsky, Noam. 2007b. Approaching UG from below. In Uli Sauerland and Hans-Martin Gärtner (eds.), *Interfaces + Recursion = Language? Chomsky's Minimalism and the View from Syntax-Semantics*, 1–29. Berlin: Mouton de Gruyter.

Chomsky, Noam. 2008. On phases. In Robert Freidin, Carlos Otero and Maria Luisa Zubizarrreta (eds.), *Foundational Issues in Linguistic Theory: Essays in Honor of Jean-Roger Vergnaud*, 291–321. Cambridge, MA: MIT Press.

Chomsky, Noam. 2010. Some simple evo-devo theses: How true might they be for language? In Richard Larson, Viviane Déprez and Hiroko Yamakido (eds.), *The Evolution of Human Language: Biolinguistic Perspectives*, 45–62. Cambridge: Cambridge University Press.

Chomsky, Noam. 2012. Poverty of the stimulus: Willingness to be puzzled. In Massimo Piattelli-Palmarini and Robert Berwick (eds.), *Rich Languages from Poor Inputs*, 61–67. Oxford: Oxford University Press.

Chomsky, Noam. 2013. Problems of projection. *Lingua* 130, 33–49.

Chomsky, Noam. 2014. Minimal recursion: Exploring the prospects. In Tom Roeper and Margaret Speas (eds.), *Recursion: Complexity in Cognition*, 1–15. Berlin: Springer.

Chomsky, Noam. 2015a. Preface to the 20th anniversary edition. In *The Minimalist Program 20th Anniversary Edition*, vii–xiv. Cambridge, MA: MIT Press.

Chomsky, Noam. 2015b. Problems of projection: extensions. In Elisa Di Domenico, Cornelia Hamann and Simona Matteini (eds.), *Structures, Strategies and Beyond: Studies in Honour of Adriana Belletti*, 3–16. Amsterdam and Philadelphia: John Benjamins.

Chomsky, Noam. 2015c. A discussion with Naoki Fukui and Mihoko Zushi (March 4, 2014). In *The Sophia lectures* (*Sophia Linguistica* 64), 69–97. Tokyo: Sophia Linguistic Institute for International Communication, Sophia University.

Chomsky, Noam, Gallego, Ángel, and Dennis Ott. 2019. Generative grammar and the faculty of language: Insights, questions, and challenges. *Catalan Journal of Linguistics Special Issue 2019*, 229–261.

Chomsky, Noam, and Howard Lasnik. 1993. The theory of principles and parameters. In Joachim Jacobs, Armin von Stechow, Wolfgang Sternefeld and Theo Vennemann (eds.), *Syntax: An International Handbook of Contemporary Research*, Vol. 1, 506–569. Berlin: Walter de Gruyter.

Clahsen, Harald. 2008. Chomskyan syntactic theory and language disorders. In Martin Ball, Michael Perkins, Nicole Müller and Sara Howard (eds.), *The Handbook of Clinical Linguistics*, 165–183. Oxford: Blackwell.

Crain, Stephen, and Diane Lillo-Martin. 1999. *An Introduction to Linguistic Theory and Language Acquisition*. Oxford: Blackwell.

Epstein, Samuel, Kitahara, Hisatsugu, and Daniel Seely. 2012. Structure building that can't be. In Myriam Uribe-Etxebarria and Vidal Valmala (eds.), *Ways of Structure Building*, 253–270. Oxford: Oxford University Press.

Fiebach, Christian, Schlesewsky, Matthias, Lohmann, Gabriele, von Cramon, Yves, and Friederici Angela. 2005. Revisiting the role of Broca's area in sentence processing: Syntactic integration versus syntactic working memory. *Human Brain Mapping* 24(2), 79–91.

Friedmann, Na'ama, and Yosef Grodzinsky. 1997. Tense and agreement in agrammatic production: Pruning the syntactic tree. *Brain and Language*, 56(3), 397–425.

Fujita, Gen. 2010. Transfer it from syntax!: A multiple Transfer analysis of the multiple nominative construction in Japanese. MA Thesis, Sophia University.

Fukuda, Shin. 2012. Aspectual verbs as functional heads: Evidence from Japanese aspectual verbs. *Natural Language & Linguistic Theory* 30(4), 965–1026.

Fukui, Naoki. 1986/1995. A theory of category projection and its applications. Doctoral dissertation, MIT. Published in 1995 with revisions as *Theory of Projection in Syntax*. Stanford: Kurosio Publishers and CSLI publications.

Fukui, Naoki. 1988. Deriving the differences between English and Japanese: A case study in parametric syntax. *English Linguistics* 5, 249–270.

Fukui, Naoki. 1990. Problems of the phrase structure of Japanese: A historical survey.

In Masashi Sakamoto and Yasuaki Abe (eds.), *Proceedings of the International Symposium on Japanese Teaching*, 261–272. Nagoya: Nanzan University.

Fukui, Naoki. 1995. The principles-and-parameters approach: A comparative syntax of English and Japanese. In Masayoshi Shibatani and Theodora Bynon (eds.), *Approaches to Language Typology*, 327–372. Oxford: Oxford University Press.

Fukui, Naoki. 1999. The uniqueness parameter. *Glot international*, 4(9–10), 26–27.

Fukui, Naoki. 2006. *Theoretical Comparative Syntax: Studies in Macroparameters*. Abingdon: Routledge.

Fukui, Naoki. 2011. Merge and bare phrase structure. In Cedric Boeckx (ed.), *The Oxford Handbook of Linguistic Minimalism*, 73–95. Oxford: Oxford University Press.

Fukui, Naoki. 2013. Seiseibumpoo to ningengengo-no "tayoosei" [Generative Grammar and the "diversity" of human language]. *Nihon Edward Sapir Kyookai Kenkyuu Nempoo* 27, 1–23.

Fukui, Naoki, and Hironobu Kasai. 2004. Spelling-out scrambling. In Pierre Pica, Johan Rooryck and Jeroen van Craenenbroeck (eds.), *Linguistic Variation Yearbook* 4(1), 109–141. Amsterdam: John Benjamins.

Fukui, Naoki, and Hiroki Narita. 2012/2017. Merge and (a)symmetry. An extended written-up version of the presentation at the Kyoto conference on Biolinguistics (March 2012). Published in Fukui, Naoki. 2017. *Merge in the Mind-Brain: Essays on Theoretical Linguistics and the Neuroscience of Language*, 35–74. Abingdon: Routledge.

Fukui, Naoki, and Taisuke Nishigauchi. 1992. Head movement and case-marking in Japanese. *Journal of Japanese Linguistics* 14(1), 1–36.

Fukui, Naoki, and Hiromu Sakai. 2003. The visibility guideline for functional categories: Verb raising in Japanese and related issues. *Lingua* 113, 321–375.

Fukushima, Kazuhiko. 2005. Lexical VV compounds in Japanese: Lexicon vs. syntax. *Language* 81(3) 568–612.

George, Leland, and Jaklin Kornfilt. 1981. Finiteness and boundedness in Turkish. In Frank Heny (ed.), *Binding and Filtering*, 105–127. Cambridge, MA: MIT Press.

Grodzinsky, Yosef. 1984. The syntactic characterization of agrammatism. *Cognition* 16(2), 99–120.

Grohmann, Kleanthes. 2011. Anti-locality: Too-close relations in grammar. In Cedric Boeckx (ed.), *The Oxford Handbook of Linguistic Minimalism*, 260–290. Oxford: Oxford University Press.

Hagiwara, Hiroko. 1995. The breakdown of functional categories and the economy of derivation. *Brain and Language* 50(1), 92–116.

Hankamer, Jorge, and Ivan Sag. 1976. Deep and surface anaphora. *Linguistic Inquiry* 7(3), 391–428.

Harada, Naomi. 2002. Licensing PF-visible formal features: A linear algorithm and case-related phenomena in PF. Doctoral dissertation, University of California, Irvine.

Harada, Shin-Ichi. 1971. Ga-no conversion and idiolectal variations in Japanese. *Gengo*

Kenkyu 60, 25–38.

Harada, Shin-Ichi. 1973. Counter equi NP deletion. *Annual Bulletin, Research Institute of Logopedics and Phoniatrics, University of Tokyo* 7, 113–147.

Harada, Shin-Ichi. 1976. Ga-no conversion revisited. *Gengo Kenkyu* 70, 23–38.

Harbour, Daniel. 2016. *Impossible Persons*. Cambridge, MA: MIT Press.

Hiraiwa, Ken. 2001. On nominative-genitive conversion. In Elena Guerzoni and Ora Matushansky (eds.), *A Few from Building E39*, 65–123. Cambridge, MA: MITWPL.

Hiraiwa, Ken. 2005. Dimensions of symmetry in syntax: Agreement and clausal architecture. Doctoral dissertation, MIT.

Hirata, Ichiro. 2011. Nihongo-no kukoozoo: Jutsugo-no tooikoozoo-o tegakari-ni. [Phrase structure in Japanese: Using predicate coordination as a clue]. Doctoral dissertation, University of Tsukuba.

Hoji, Hajime. 1998. Null object and sloppy identity in Japanese. *Linguistic Inquiry* 29(1), 127–152.

Huang, C.-T. James. 1984. On the distribution and reference of empty pronouns. *Linguistic Inquiry* 15(4), 531–574.

Ito, Katsumasa. 2018. Doitsugo-no w-kantanbun-ni okeru dooshi-no ichi-to sono-imiron [The place of verbs and the semantics of w-exclamatives in German]. *Language and Information Sciences* 16, 1–17.

Jayaseelan, K. A. 1999. *Parametric Studies in Malayalam Syntax*. New Delhi: Allied Publishers.

Jordens, Peter. 2002. Finiteness in early child Dutch. *Linguistics* 40 (4): 687–766.

Kageyama, Taro. 1993. *Bunpoo to Gokeesei* [*Grammar and Word Formation*]. Tokyo: Hituzi Syobo Publishing.

Kageyama, Taro. 2016. Verb-compounding and verb-incorporation. In Taro Kageyama and Hideki Kishimoto (eds.), *Handbook of Japanese Lexicon and Word Formation*, 273–310. Berlin: Walter de Gruyter GmbH & Co KG.

Kayne, Richard. 2003. Silent years, silent hours. In Lars-Olof Delsing, Gunlög Josefsson, Halldor Armann Sigurðsson and Cecilia Falk (eds.), *Grammar in Focus: Festschrift for Christer Platzack*, 209–226. Lund: Wallin and Dalholm.

Kayne, Richard. 2016. The silence of heads. *Studies in Chinese Linguistics* 37(1), 1–37.

Khurelbat, Pandzragchin. 1992. Word formation in Mongolian language. Doctoral dissertation, Jawaharlal Nehru University.

Kim, Soowon. 1999. Sloppy / strict identity, empty objects, and NP ellipsis. *Journal of East Asian Linguistics* 8(4), 255–284.

Ko, Heejeong, and Daeyoung Sohn. 2015. Decomposing complex serialization: The role of *v*. *Korean Linguistics* 17(1), 78–125.

Kobayashi, Yukino. 2012. Anti-licensing theory of unmarked cases and ga / no conversion. In Nobu Goto, Koichi Otaki, Atsushi Sato and Kensuke Takita (eds.), *Online Proceedings of GLOW in Asia IX 2012*, 1–13. Mie: Mie University.

Kobayashi, Ryoichiro. 2018a. Parametrizing the timing of Transfer in Japanese and

English and its consequences. In Céleste Guillemot, Tomoyuki Yoshida and Seunghun J. Lee (eds.), *Proceedings of the 13th Workshop on Altaic Formal Linguistics*, 371–379. Cambridge, MA: MITWPL.

Kobayashi, Ryoichiro. 2018b. Feature Inheritance and the Syntax of Lexical VV Compounds. In Kate Bellamy, Anastasiia Ionova and George Saad (eds.), *Proceedings of the ConSOLE XXV*, 250–267. Leiden: Leiden University Centre for Linguistics.

Kobayashi, Ryoichiro. 2021. Labeling the unlabelable in the CP domain. In Sho Akamine (ed.), *Proceedings of the 32nd Western Conference on Linguistics*, 1–10. Fresno: California State University.

Kobayashi, Ryoichiro. 2022. Functional parametrization hypothesis in the minimalist program. Doctoral dissertation, Sophia University.

Krishnamurti, Bhadriraju. 2003. *The Dravidian Languages*. Cambridge: Cambridge University Press.

Kuno, Susumu. 1973. *The Structure of the Japanese Language*. Cambridge, MA: MIT Press.

Kuno, Susumu, and Etsuko Kaburaki. 1977. Empathy and syntax. *Linguistic Inquiry*, 8(4), 627–672.

Kuribayashi, Yu. 2006. Torukogo-no hukugoodooshi to bumpooka. [Compound verbs and their grammaticalization in Turkish]. *Azia, Ahurika-no Gengo to Gengogaku*, 1, 25–44.

Kuroda, Shige-Yuki. 1973. On Kuno's direct discourse analysis of the Japanese reflexive zibun. *Papers in Japanese Linguistics* 2(1), 136–147.

Kuroda, Shige-Yuki. 1988. Whether we agree or not: a comparative syntax of English and Japanese. *Lingvisticae Investigationes*, 12(1), 1–47.

Lebeaux, David. 1988. Language acquisition and the form of the grammar. Doctoral dissertation, University of Massachusetts, Amherst.

Lebeaux, David. 2000. *Language Acquisition and the Form of the Grammar*. Amsterdam: John Benjamins.

Lewontin, Richard. 1985. Adaptation. In Richard Levins and Richard Lewontin (eds.), *The Dialectical Biologist*, 65–84. Cambridge, MA: Harvard University Press.

Li, Charles, and Sandra Thompson. 1976. Subject and topic: A new typology of language. In Charles Li (ed.), *Subject and Topic*, 457–489. New York: Academic Press.

Lieber, Rochelle. 2005. English word-formation processes. In Pavol Štekauer and Rochelle Lieber (eds.), *Handbook of Word-formation*, 375–427. Netherlands: Springer.

Lillo-Martin, Diane. 1994. Setting the null argument parameters: Evidence from American Sign Language and other languages. In Barbara Lust, Gabriella Hermon and Jaklin Kornfilt (eds.), *Syntactic Theory and First Language Acquisition: Cross-linguistic Perspectives Vol. 2: Binding, Dependencies, and Learnability*, 301–318. Hillsdale, NJ: Erlbaum.

Maki, Hideki, and Asako Uchibori. 2008. Ga / no conversion. In Shigeru Miyagawa and Mamoru Saito (eds.), *Handbook of Japanese Linguistics*, 192–216. Oxford: Oxford University Press.

Manzini, Rita, and Kenneth Wexler. 1987. Parameters, binding theory, and learnability. *Linguistic Inquiry* 18(3), 413–444.

McGinnis, Martha. 2001. Phases and the syntax of applicatives. In Minjoo Kim and Uri Strauss (eds.), *Proceedings of the 31ˢᵗ Meeting of the North East Linguistic Society*, 333–349. Amherst: University of Massachusetts, GLSA.

McGinnis, Martha. 2002. Object asymmetries in a phase theory of Syntax. Paper presented at the 2001 CLA Annual Conference, Cahiers Linguistiques d'Ottawa.

Miyagawa, Shigeru. 2010. *Why Agree? Why Move?* Cambridge, MA: MIT Press.

Miyagawa, Shigeru. 2017. *Agreement beyond Phi.* Cambridge, MA: MIT Press.

Muysken, Pieter. 2008. *Functional Categories.* Cambridge: Cambridge University Press.

Nagamori, Takakazu. 2020. Multiple case valuation via agree / merge. Doctoral dissertation, Sophia University.

Nakao, Hisashi. 2012. Seibutsu shinka-to bunka shinka-ni okeru mojuurusei [Modularity in biological and cultural evolution]. *Kagaku Kisoron Kenkyu* 40(1), 1–8.

Nakao, Hisashi. 2013. Shinkashinrigaku-no yougo—Hihan-no hanbaku-o tsuujite [Defending evolutionary psychology through rebutting the criticisms]. *Kagaku Tetsugaku* 46(1), 1–16.

Narita, Hiroki. 2014. *Endocentric Structuring of Projection-free Syntax.* Amsterdam: John Benjamins.

Narita, Hiroki, and Naoki Fukui. 2022. *Symmetrizing Syntax: Merge, Minimality, and Equilibria.* Abingdon: Routledge.

Neef, Martin. 2009. IE, Germanic: German. In Rochelle Lieber and Pavol Štekauer (eds.). *The Oxford Handbook of Compounding*, 386–399. Oxford: Oxford University Press.

Neeleman, Ad, and Hans van de Koot. 2006. Syntactic haplology. In Martin Everaert and Henk van Riemsdijk (eds.), *The Blackwell Companion to Syntax Vol. 4* (First Edition), 685–710. London: Wiley-Blackwell.

Nemoto, Naoko. 1999. Scrambling. In Natsuko Tsujimura (ed.), *The Handbook of Japanese Linguistics*, 121–153. Oxford: Blackwell.

Newson, Mark. 1990. Dependencies in the lexical setting of parameters: A solution to the undergeneralization problem. In Iggy Roca (ed.), *Logical Issues in Language Acquisition*, 177–198. Dordrecht: Foris.

Niinuma, Fumikazu. 2003. The syntax of honorification. Doctoral dissertation, University of Connecticut.

Nishiyama, Kunio. 1998. VV compounds as serialization. *Journal of East Asian Linguistics* 7(3), 175–217.

Nishiyama, Kunio. 2008. V-V compounds. In Shigeru Miyagawa and Mamoru Saito (eds.), *Handbook of Japanese Linguistics*, 320–347. Oxford: Oxford University Press.

Nishiyama, Kunio, and Yoshiki Ogawa. 2014. Auxiliation, atransitivity, and transitivity harmony in Japanese VV compounds. *Interdisciplinary Information Sciences*, 20(2), 71–101.

Nitta, Yoshio. 1991. *Nihongo-no Modaritii-to Ninsyoo.* [*Modality and Person in Japanese*]. Tokyo: Hituzi Syobo Publishing.

Obata, Miki. 2010. Root, successive-cyclic and feature-splitting internal merge: Implications for feature-inheritance and transfer. Doctoral dissertation, University of Michigan.

Obata, Miki, and Mina Sugimura. 2014. Phi-agreement in Japanese: On the person restriction of Case valuation. In Claire Renaud, Carla Ghanem, Verónica González López and Kathryn Pruitt (eds.), *Proceedings of the 40th Western Conference on Linguistics*, 111–119. Fresno: California State University.

Obata, Miki, and Mina Sugimura. 2019. Phi-agreement by C in Japanese: Evidence from person restriction on the subject. In Ryo Otoguro, Mamoru Komachi and Tomoko Ohkuma (eds.), *Proceedings of the 33rd Pacific Asia Conference on Language, Information and Computation*, 191–195. Tokyo: Waseda Institute for the Study of Language and Information.

Ochi, Masao. 2001. Move F and ga / no conversion in Japanese. *Journal of East Asian Linguistics* 10(3), 247–286.

Oku, Satoshi. 1998. A theory of selection and reconstruction in the minimalist perspective. Doctoral dissertation, University of Connecticut.

Otsuka, Jun. 2007. Kekkyoku, kinoo-to-wa nan-dat-ta-no-ka [Reconciling two concepts of function]. *Kagaku Tetsugaku* 40(1), 29–40.

Paschen, Ludger. 2014. Opacity in the lexicon: A generative lexicon approach to Korean VV compounds. In Anke Assmann, Sebastian Bank, Doreen Georgi, Timo Klein, Philipp Weisser and Eric Zimmermann (eds.), *Topics at Infl*, 197–234. Universität Leipzig.

Paul, Soma. 2003. Composition of compound verbs in Bangla. In Dorothee Beermann and Lars Hellan (eds.), *Proceedings of the Workshop on Multi-verb Constructions*, 1–18. Trondheim: Norwegian University of Science and Technology.

Paul, Waltraud. 2017. Null subject, null topics and topic prominence in Mandarin Chinese and beyond. In Si Fuzhen (ed.), *Studies on Syntactic Cartography*, 391–420. Beijing: Chinese Social Sciences Academy Press.

Penke, Martine. 1998. *Die Grammatik des Agrammatismus*. Niemeyer: Tubingen.

Penke, Martine. 2000. Unpruned trees in German Broca's aphasia. *Behavioral and Brain Sciences* 23, 46–47.

Platzack, Christer. 1990. A grammar without functional categories: A syntactic study of early Swedish child language. *Nordic Journal of Linguistics* 13(2), 107–126.

Poeppel, David, and Kenneth Wexler 1993. The full competence hypothesis of clause structure in early German. *Language* 69(1), 1–33.

Potts, Christopher, and Tom Roeper. 2006. The narrowing acquisition path: From expressive small clauses to declaratives. In Ljiljana Progovac, Kate Paesani, Eugenia Casielles and Ellen Barton (eds.), *The Syntax of Nonsententials*, 183–201.

Amsterdam: John Benjamins.

Preminger, Omer. 2014. *Agreement and its Failures*. Cambridge, MA: MIT Press.

Progovac, Ljiljana. 2015. *Evolutionary Syntax*. Oxford: Oxford University Press.

Radford, Andrew. 1988. Small children's small clauses. *Transactions of the Philological Society* 86(1), 1–43.

Radford, Andrew. 1990. *Syntactic Theory and the Acquisition of English Syntax: The Nature of Early Child Grammars of English*. Cambridge, MA: Basil Blackwell.

Richards, Marc. 2007. On feature inheritance: An argument from the Phase Impenetrability Condition. *Linguistic Inquiry* 38(3), 563–572.

Rizzi, Luigi. 1997. The fine structure of the left periphery. In Liliane Haegeman (ed.), *Elements of Grammar*, 281–337. Dordrecht: Kluwer.

Roberts, Ian. 2018. *Diachronic and Comparative Syntax*. New York and London: Routledge.

Roberts, Ian, and Anna Roussou. 2003. *Syntactic Change: A Minimalist Approach to Grammaticalization*. Cambridge: Cambridge University Press.

Safir, Kenneth. 1987. Comments on Wexler and Manzini. In Tom Roeper and Edwin Williams (eds.), *Parameter Setting*, 77–89. Dordrecht: Reidel.

Saito, Mamoru. 1989. Scrambling as semantically vacuous A′-movement. In Mark Baltin and Anthony Kroch (eds.), *Alternative Conceptions of Phrase Structure*, 182–200. Chicago: University of Chicago Press.

Saito, Mamoru. 1992. Long distance scrambling in Japanese. *Journal of East Asian Linguistics* 1(1), 69–118.

Saito, Mamoru. 2003. A derivational approach to the interpretation of scrambling chains. *Lingua* 113, 481–518.

Saito, Mamoru. 2007. Notes on East Asian argument ellipsis. *Language Research* 43, 203–227.

Saito, Mamoru. 2012. Case checking/valuation in Japanese: Move, Agree, or Merge. *Nanzan Linguistics* 8, 109–127.

Saito, Mamoru. 2014. Case and labeling in a language without φ-feature agreement. In Anna Cardinaletti, Guglielmo Cinque and Yoshio Endo (eds.), *On Peripheries: Exploring Clause Initial and Clause Final Positions*, 269–297. Tokyo: Hituzi Syobo Publishing.

Saito, Mamoru. 2016. (A) Case for labeling: labeling in languages without φ-feature agreement. *The Linguistic Review* 33(1), 129–175.

Saito, Mamoru, and Keiko Murasugi. 1999. Subject predication within IP and DP. In Kyle Johnson and Ian Roberts (eds.), *Beyond Principles and Parameters*, 167–188. Dordrecht: Kluwer.

Sakamoto, Yuta. 2011. A study of sluicing and cleft in Mongolian: A comparison with Japanese. MA thesis, Tohoku University.

Şener, Serkan, and Daiko Takahashi. 2010. Ellipsis of arguments in Japanese and Turkish. *Nanzan Linguistics* 6, 79–99.

Shibatani, Masayoshi. 1978a. *Nihongo-no Bunseki* [*An Analysis of Japanese*]. Tokyo: Taishukan.

Shibatani, Masayoshi. 1978b. Mikami Akira and the notion of 'subject' in Japanese grammar. In John Hinds and Irwin Howard (eds.), *Problems in Japanese Syntax and Semantics*, 52–67. Tokyo: Kaitakusha.

Shim, Jae-Young, and Samuel Epstein. 2015. Two notes on possible approaches to the unification of theta relations. *Linguistic Analysis* 40(1), 1–18.

Siddiqi, Daniel. 2010. Distributed Morphology. *Language and Linguistic Compass* 4(7), 524–542.

Tada, Hiroaki. 1993. A / A-bar partition in derivation. Doctoral dissertation, MIT.

Takahashi, Yohei. 2015. Kuusyo ketsuraku kankeisetsu-no idoo bunseki. [The movement analysis of gapless relative clauses]. In Hiroki Egashira, Hisatsugu Kitahara, Kazuo Nakazawa, Tadao Nomura, Masayuki Oishi, Akira Saizen and Motoko Suzuki (eds.), *Yori Yoki Daian-o Taezu Motomete* [*In Untiring Pursuit of Better Alternatives*], 404–412. Tokyo: Kaitakusha.

Takita, Kensuke, Goto, Nobu, and Yoshiyuki Shibata. 2016. Labeling through Spell-Out. *The Linguistic Review* 33(1), 177–198.

Tallerman, Maggie. 1990. VSO word order and consonantal mutation in Welsh. *Linguistics* 28(3), 389–416.

Thompson, Cynthia, Fix, Stephen, and Darren Gitelman. 2002. Selective impairment of morphosyntactic production in a neurological patient. *Journal of Neurolinguistics* 15(3–5), 189–207.

Thornton, Abigail. 2019. Agreeing in number: Verbal plural suppletion and reduplication. *The Linguistic Review*, 36(3), 531–552.

Thornton, Rosalind, and Graciela Tesan. 2007. Categorical acquisition: parameter-setting in Universal Grammar. *Biolinguistics* 1, 49–98.

Toribio, Almeida Jacqueline. 1990. Specifier-head agreement in Japanese. In Aaron Halpern (ed.), *Proceedings of the 9th West Coast Conference on Formal Linguistics*, 535–548. Stanford: CSLI.

Travis, Lisa. 2014. The integration, proliferation, and expansion of functional categories. In Andrew Carnie, Yosuke Sato and Daniel Siddiqi (eds.), *The Routledge handbook of Syntax*, 42–64. New York and London: Routledge.

Tsao, Fengfu. 1977. A functional study of topic in Chinese: The first step toward discourse analysis. Doctoral dissertation, University of Southern California.

Ueda, Yukiko. 2008. Person restriction and syntactic structure of Japanese modals. *Scientific Approaches to Language* 7, 123–150.

Ura, Hiroyuki. 1996. Multiple feature-checking: A theory of grammatical function splitting. Doctoral dissertation, MIT.

Ura, Hiroyuki. 2000. *Checking Theory and Grammatical Functions in Universal Grammar.* New York and Oxford: Oxford University Press.

Vikner, Sten. 1985. Parameters of binder and of binding category in Danish. *Working Papers in Scandinavian Syntax* 23, 1–61. Dragvoll, Norway: University of Trondheim.

Vitale, Anthony. 1981. *Swahili Syntax.* Berlin: Walter de Gruyter.

Walsh, Denis. 2003. Fit and diversity: Explaining adaptive evolution. *Philosophy of*

Science 70(2), 280–301.

Watanabe, Akira. 1996. Nominative-genitive conversion and agreement in Japanese: A cross-linguistic perspective. *Journal of East Asian Linguistics* 5(4), 373–410.

Wenzlaff, Michaela, and Harald Clahsen. 2005. Finiteness and verb-second in German agrammatism. *Brain and Language* 92(1), 33–44.

Wexler, Kenneth. 1998. Very early parameter setting and the unique checking constraint: a new explanation of the optional infinitive stage. *Lingua* 106, 23–79.

Wexler, Kenneth, and Rita Manzini. 1987. Parameters and learnability in binding theory. In Tom Roeper and Edwin Williams (eds.), *Parameter Setting*, 41–76. Dordrecht: Reidel.

Wurmbrand, Susi. 2000. The structure(s) of particle verbs. Ms., McGill University.

Yang, Dong-Whee. 1983. The extended binding theory of anaphors. *Language Research* 19, 169–192.

Yashima, Jun. 2008. Clausal architecture and complex predicate formation: A case study of Japanese syntactic VV compounds. MA thesis, University of Tokyo.

Zushi, Mihoko. 2003. Null arguments: The case of Japanese and Romance. *Lingua* 113, 559–604.

Zushi, Mihoko. 2014. Kaku to heigoo. [Case and merge]. In Koji Fujita, Naoki Fukui, Yusa Noriaki and Masayuki Ike-uchi (eds.), *Gengo-no Sekkei, Hattatsu, Shinka. [The Design, Development and Evolution of Language: Explorations in Biolinguistics]*, 66–96. Tokyo: Kaitakusha.

Zushi, Mihoko. 2016. Case and predicate-argument relations. In Koji Fujita and Cedric Boeckx (eds.), *Advances in Biolinguistics: The Human Language Faculty and its Biological Basis*, 46–66. New York: Routledge.

Index

Functional Parametrization Hypothesis in the Minimalist Program: Case Studies from the Perspective of Comparative Syntax of Japanese and English

著作者　　小林亮一朗
発行者　　武 村 哲 司
印刷所　　日之出印刷株式会社

2022 年 11 月 19 日　第 1 版第 1 刷発行©

発行所　　株式会社　開 拓 社

〒112-0013 東京都文京区音羽 1-22-16
電話　（03) 5395-7101（代表)
振替　00160-8-39587
http://www.kaitakusha.co.jp

ISBN978-4-7589-2378-1　C3080

|JCOPY| ＜出版者著作権管理機構 委託出版物＞
本書の無断複製は，著作権法上での例外を除き禁じられています．複製される場合は，そのつど事前に，
出版者著作権管理機構（電話 03-5244-5088, FAX 03-5244-5089, e-mail: info@jcopy.or.jp）の許諾を
得てください．